FOCUS ON THE FAMILY®

Tyndale House Publishers, Inc.
Carol Stream, Illinois

ALEX McFARLAND

STAND

unleashing the WISDOM of God

Stand: Unleashing the Wisdom of God
Copyright © 2009 by Alex McFarland
All rights reserved. International copyright secured.

A Focus on the Family book published by
Tyndale House Publishers, Inc., Carol Stream, Illinois 60188.

Focus on the Family and the accompanying logo and design
are federally registered trademarks of Focus on the Family,
Colorado Springs, CO 80995.

TYNDALE and Tyndale's quill logo are registered trademarks
of Tyndale House Publishers, Inc.

All Scripture quotations, unless otherwise indicated, are
taken from the *Holy Bible, New International Version®*. NIV®.
Copyright © 1973, 1978, 1984 by International Bible Society.
Used by permission of Zondervan Publishing House. All rights
reserved.

Italics or bold in quoted verses were added by the author for
emphasis.

People's names and certain details of their stories have been
changed to protect the privacy of the individuals involved.
However, the facts of what happened and the underlying principles have been conveyed as accurately as possible.

The use of material from various Web sites does not imply
endorsement of those sites in their entirety.

Editor: Marianne Hering
Cover design: Erik M. Peterson
Cover photo of tree copyright © by Image 100 Photography/
Veer. All rights reserved.
Cover design copyright © by You Work for Them, LLC. All rights
reserved.

Printed in the United States of America
1 2 3 4 5 6 7 8 9 / 14 13 12 11 10 09

ISBN-10: 1-58997-484-0
ISBN-13: 978-1-58997-484-5

Dedicated to
Shawn and Buck

CONTENTS

INTRODUCTION

Before there were rock stars there was . . . Solomon.

Seriously, he was a superstar in his own time. He was the definition of popular. Kings came from around the world to meet with him because he was so smart, a walking Wikipedia. How did he get celebrity status for being scholarly? Let me tell you.

As a young man, Solomon was passionate about learning (see Ecclesiastes 1:13; 1 Kings 3:9–12). He was able to speak intelligently about subjects as wide-ranging as botany, zoology, science, business, and politics. Not only did Solomon seek knowledge of the world, but he also sought to understand God's Words. This pursuit will sharpen your mind, train your will, and direct your emotions. Seeking God and His wisdom is what made Solomon a superstar.

When I think of men who were both godly and wise, I think of "Tommy's." The gas station was an auto-mechanic shop with two rusty gas pumps out front and a porch that ran along the entire front of the small building. It looked like a set from an old movie. Inside was a wooden floor made of long, narrow boards that creaked when you walked across them. Next to shelves of dust-covered car accessories was an icebox filled with Popsicles and soda. When the sun was streaming in the windows just right, you could see a well-worn path on the floor made by countless people who had passed that way to get something cold to eat or drink.

Tommy's was about three quarters of a mile from my farming neighborhood, and my friends and I rode bikes there on many a summer day to buy Cokes in glass bottles. Before starting back, we stood under the shade of the porch to rest, sip our sodas, and listen to the old, wise men.

Even in the coldest winter months, at least one or two of the neighborhood philosophers would be there on that porch. One day it dawned on me that these old guys weren't just wasting time until they died of boredom; they were sharing their smarts with each other and with anyone who was eavesdropping.

When I was a boy, I didn't know that most of those men were Christians. But when I began to attend church in my college years, I recognized some of the old faces from Tommy's gas station in the congregation. I found out they included a college professor, entrepreneurs, war veterans, successful business people, and a local attorney who had served as a congressman.

I learned that the source of their wisdom was God.

Wisdom is the ability to see life from God's point of view. Many of the men who sat in front of Tommy's all those years ago understood that. The book of Proverbs can teach you the same thing— and you don't even have to travel to Tommy's and stand on the porch!

As you make friends, choose a vocation, learn

about your spiritual gifts, and mature and move toward adulthood, the book of Proverbs can help you grow in the ways of wisdom. Wisdom will guide you in all areas of your life, from dating to driving, from pimples to politics, from gawkiness to godliness.

SOLOMON'S BIOGRAPHY

We know that Solomon was one of King David's sons and that he built the first temple at Jerusalem. His mother was Bathsheba, and he came to the throne after much bloodshed. Huge sections of the Bible (1 Kings 1–11 and 2 Chronicles 1–9) describe him and his reign as king. We even know some odd things about him, such as the fact that he collected apes and baboons for his personal zoo (see 1 Kings 10:22). And though he's one of the most famous men in all of history, parts of his life are a mystery. The more we know about Solomon, the more we realize how complex his personality and character were.

As an introduction to some of Solomon's positive qualities, let's look at 1 Kings 4:29-34:

> God gave Solomon wisdom and very great insight, and a breadth of understanding as measureless as the sand on the seashore. Solomon's wisdom was greater than the wisdom of all the men of the East, and greater than all of Egypt. He was wiser than any other man. . . . And his fame spread to all the surrounding nations. He spoke three

thousand proverbs and his songs numbered a thousand and five. He described plant life, from the cedar of Lebanon to the hyssop that grows out of walls. He also taught about animals and birds, reptiles and fish. Men of all nations came to listen to Solomon's wisdom, sent by all the kings of the world, who had heard of his wisdom.

Though his fame is undisputed, Solomon had blatant flaws that surfaced near the end of his life. Like a wild rock star, he had a voracious appetite for women and wealth. He kept 300 concubines and 700 wives, some of whom he married to consolidate his political power, and some of whom he married because he found them physically attractive (see 1 Kings 11:1-6; Nehemiah 13:26). He heavily taxed the people to finance extravagant buildings, such as a horse stable with 4,000 stalls (see 2 Chronicles 10:4; 1 Kings 4:26). He also used slave labor and allowed the workers to be whipped (see 1 Kings 4:21; 9:15, 21; 2 Chronicles 10:14).

As wise as Solomon was—and indeed, many of his proverbs warn against sexual sin and greed—his right thinking didn't always translate to right actions. But just because human role models fail, it doesn't mean that we can't learn from them. The Bible tells of many followers of God—like Abraham, Moses, Joseph, Peter, and Paul—who made mistakes but turned back to Him and remained faithful to the end. God's power and wisdom are available to us, and with His help we can choose a holy path.

Jesus and Solomon

Jesus quoted or paraphrased the proverbs many times. He considered them valuable for teaching even though He knew the author, Solomon, had some serious sin issues. Check out how similar these two passages are:

> A man's pride brings him low, but a man of lowly spirit gains honor. (Solomon in Proverbs 29:23)

> For whoever exalts himself will be humbled, and whoever humbles himself will be exalted. (Jesus in Matthew 23:12)

If Jesus respected the teachings, so can we. Also compare Proverbs 4:18-19 and John 12:35; Proverbs 4:23 and Matthew 12:34; Proverbs 8:32 and Luke 11:28; Proverbs 21:2 and Luke 16:15; Proverbs 29:13 and Matthew 5:45.

Solomon's failures may make you angry. But don't let that anger spoil your appreciation and reverence for the proverbs he wrote or compiled. Consider the following truths:

1. A teacher and a Savior are two separate things. The only true, 100-percent trustworthy hero in the Bible was Jesus. Jesus, as the unique Son of God, was the only man to perfectly live what He preached. The life of Solomon shows us that wisdom isn't enough for salvation and right living. We need Jesus to save us and forgive us when we sin. We also need God's Spirit to guide us daily so that we can clean up our lives. Praise God we have both a Savior and the Holy Spirit to help us.

2. Knowing and doing are two separate things.
Knowing the truth doesn't necessarily mean that
we always follow the truth. We must guard our
hearts. If a man as wise and great as Solomon could
be led astray, we're vulnerable to making big mistakes as well. Admitting that we aren't perfect is
the first step toward gaining wisdom (we'll touch
on humility later in the book).

*3. Preaching and practicing are two separate
things.* Solomon didn't fully practice what he
preached, but that doesn't mean his preaching was
wrong or bad. For example, Jesus said this about
the Pharisees:

> The teachers of the law and the Pharisees sit
> in Moses' seat. So you must obey them and do
> everything they tell you. But do not do what
> they do, for they do not practice what they
> preach. (Matthew 23:2-3)

It's always better if people practice what they
preach, but the preaching and the practicing
should be evaluated separately. So let's forgive
Solomon for his flaws and at the same time cling
to what we can learn from his trustworthy writing.

Now let's look at some of Solomon's powerful
preaching.

1

PERSPECTIVE

what does God think is important?

You've probably heard the expression "bird's-eye view." It means having an elevated position, seeing the big picture. A bald eagle soars over hills and valleys, seeing the whole landscape. But it can also zero in on ground details; it can spot a rabbit moving a mile away. Eagle eyes also have two points of focus, which means they can look forward and to the side at the same time. With such great vision, an eagle flying at 1,000 feet over open land can identify small animals over an area of almost three square miles.

The book of Proverbs gives us better than a bird's-eye view; it gives us a "God's-eye" view, an eternal outlook on life. Proverbs are about seeing the world as God sees it, having God's mind. That perspective is called wisdom.

HOW WE'LL STUDY PROVERBS

The book of Proverbs is like a great musical work. The most famous musical masterpieces, the simplest children's songs, even the bleats and squeaks of an orchestra warming up are made up of the same 12 individual notes of the chromatic scale. What makes one piece high art and the other merely distracting noise is how the notes are put together.

At first glance, the individual notes—or verses—of Proverbs may seem simple and familiar. Proverbs is full of advice, often presented as one-liners. These one-liners are like the "Da, Da, Da, DUM!" of Beethoven's Fifth Symphony. They're memorable and dramatic. Consider Proverbs 26:20, for example:

> Without wood a fire goes out;
>> without gossip a quarrel dies down.

These one-liners are often repeated and actually blend with each other. I believe you'll end up not only being able to hear all the individual parts of Proverbs, but you'll also be able to put them together in a harmonious way that will give your life direction—God's big-picture perspective.

MY PERSPECTIVE ON THE WORDS OF GOD

Let's face it, some passages of Scripture are easier to dig into than others. Proverbs is one of those simple-to-understand books because it's plain and direct. Right at the beginning of the book, we get the message:

> The proverbs of Solomon son of David, king of Israel: for attaining wisdom and discipline. (1:1-2)

Proverbs fast facts

- The book of Proverbs has 31 chapters.
- Chapters are divided into phrases.
- A phrase is 2 to 10 verses.
- A phrase is a complete thought.
- If a phrase is repeated, it adds a new insight.

Solomon goes on to say that the Proverbs has a particular audience as well: the "young" (1:4). Indeed, the first third of Proverbs is wisdom condensed and applicable for teens. For you.

The book of Proverbs contains the Words of God. That expression, *the Words of God*, means something very specific to me, and I want to define it here so we all understand that perspective. Most Christian pastors and teachers would agree with the core statements I make in the following sections, yet a few would quibble here and there with my word choices or emphases. But I think all Christian scholars would agree that the Words of God contain the wisdom of God and are therefore worthy of the most scrutinizing study and devotion.

The Words of God are inerrant

I believe God's Words are inerrant or "without error." Therefore, the original manuscripts of the Bible are free from all contradiction and are accurate in the historical and scientific facts they present.

However, inerrancy doesn't mean that every word in the Bible is to be taken literally. Some passages

Why is Proverbs part of the Bible?

There are thousands of proverbs or maxims dating back as far as the twenty-fifth century b.c. what made Solomon's collection so special that it was included in the Bible?

The first reason christians believe that Proverbs is holy stems from its historical acceptance in the God-fearing community. From ancient times to today, Jewish Leaders have viewed Proverbs as scripture. Additionally, Jesus assigned authority to Proverbs by quoting from it several times. Early christian Leaders also affirmed that the proverbs were divine writings.

Second, the content of Proverbs is compatible with the rest of the Bible. It rings true and is undeniably deep and profound. Not all ancient books of the Bible are meant to be read as poetry or figuratively. Consider Proverbs 30:17:

> The eye that mocks a father,
>   that scorns obedience to a mother,
> will be pecked out by the ravens of the valley,
>   will be eaten by the vultures.

Does this passage mean that every person who has ever mocked his father will one day be found with vacant eye sockets, dead in a valley with vultures feasting upon his flesh? No. This passage is obviously a metaphor. It means that the person who continually mocks his parents will come to great trouble and leave behind a wasted life.

that are consistent with the Bible had such obvious value.

And that leads us to the third reason Proverbs made the grade—it exhibits life-changing power. Proverbs is part of a collection of writings called wisdom literature. The book's goals are to expand your mind, enhance your life, and contribute toward the saving of your soul. Why not test it and see if it delivers?

Because the book of Proverbs is inerrant, authoritative, and inspired by God, if you follow its teachings, odds are your life will go better in spiritual areas. Proverbs offers us insight into how the world works so that we can understand the inevitable order of the world that springs from the mind of God.

Other literary devices are used in Scripture. For example, Proverbs 30 uses an expression that seems odd when first encountered:

> There are three things that are never satisfied,
>   four that never say, "Enough!" (verse 15)

A few verses later, we read,

> There are three things that are too amazing for me,
>   four that I do not understand. (verse 18)

This figure of speech—using the numbers three and four—is repeated several more times in Proverbs. Why? The answer is that this expression is a literary device. In the South, when someone has an outlandish story to tell, he'll sometimes begin with "Y'all ain't gonna believe this!" In a way, that's what the writer, Agur, was doing. (More on Agur in chapter 10.) He was using a poetic expression that communicates this idea: "There are certain things in the world that are just too marvelous for words. Here are a few, but they are by no means all."

A metaphor is a word picture that makes a point.

Since my entire manuscript encourages you to trust the Bible for wisdom, instruction, and doctrine, it's only fair that we spend a few minutes on this question: How do we know that we can trust the Bible? Let me make two quick points in response.

1. The Bible claims to be trustworthy. Consider Proverbs 30:5 as exhibit A in this argument:

> Every word of God is flawless; he is a shield
> to those who take refuge in him.

Just because someone says that he or she is trustworthy doesn't necessarily make that person trustworthy. However, imagine your friend saying that tomorrow night the full moon will disappear from the sky. You'd think he was crazy, right? But what if your friend was an astronomer, and his calculations showed there would be an eclipse? In that case, you'd likely believe him.

So it is with the Bible. The Bible doesn't just say

it's flawless. It contains a great deal of information about life and human history that we know to be true. Scripture has stood the challenges and attacks against it through the ages. When those challenges against the Bible are seriously examined, they don't hold up. Outside sources confirm and validate the Bible's claims. Billions of people over thousands of years have found the Bible to be trustworthy and true. When the Bible calls itself "flawless," it's a claim we can trust.

2. God reveals Himself through the Bible. God's character and greatness are far beyond human understanding. We can know only what God wants us to know about Him. That's why Christianity is a "revealed" religion. God reveals Himself in two ways: special revelation and general revelation.

Special revelation is the way God reaches out to us. The Bible, Jesus' life, and the presence of the Holy Spirit are three elements of God's special revelation to humankind.

General revelation is seen through creation. The design, beauty, and vastness of the world leave humankind with a sense of God, or "God-consciousness." The apostle Paul, in Romans 1:20, put it this way: "For since the creation of the world God's invisible qualities—his eternal power and divine nature—have been clearly seen, being understood from what has been made, so that men are without excuse." Proverbs 30:24-31 encourages us to look closely at the natural world and appreciate God's creation.

Hey! How'd that get there?

There's an old saying you'll sometimes hear in the south: "If you see a turtle on a fence post, you may not be able to say how it got there, but you can be pretty sure it didn't get there by itself." By looking at the world around us, we can see that the complex things in it didn't get there by themselves; they must have had a creator.

The Words of God are authoritative

Christians look to the Words of God as the highest and best source of spiritual direction and church teaching, called doctrine. For that reason, when Bible scholars try to figure out what a certain passage of Scripture means, their first source of comparison is other passages of Scripture. In other words, Bible scholars first let scripture teach scripture. Then they take into account other principles.

Fancy word alert: Hermeneutics means "how we understand scripture."

The Words of God are inspired

When I mention that Solomon wrote and compiled Proverbs, this statement has a deeper meaning. God gave Solomon wisdom, and Solomon wrote down the words with His help and direction. In the Bible the word *inspiration* means "God-breathed" (see 1 Thessalonians 2:13 and 2 Timothy 3:16-17). This signifies that the Bible contains the very

Words of God, His perspective on life. I believe that God helped the human authors of the Scriptures in such a way that what they wrote were the very Words of God—but the writers weren't robots. God used each one individually and allowed each one his own style.

The content of the Bible wasn't chosen by men; it was given by God.

Proverbs have more significance than pithy sayings such as "An apple a day keeps the doctor away." The book of Proverbs is God's wisdom to man; it's eternal, spiritual, and irrefutable.

Listening to God's perspective

Let the wise listen and add to their learning.
(Proverbs 1:5)
Whoever listens to me will live in safety. (1:33)
Listen, my sons, to a father's instruction;
pay attention and gain understanding. (4:1)
Listen to my instruction and be wise. (8:33)
Blessed is the man who listens to me, watching daily
at my doors, waiting at my doorway. (8:34)
The way of a fool seems right to him,
but a wise man listens to advice. (12:15)
A mocker does not listen to rebuke. (13:1)

2

WISDOM

what is more valuable than money?

One of the most famous sculptures in the world is named *The Thinker*, created by Auguste Rodin in the early 1900s. It's a bronze and marble statue of a seated man; his elbow is on his knee, and his chin is resting on the palm of his hand. *The Thinker* has come to represent a man in deep contemplation, a philosophical soul. Rodin once said, "I choose a block of marble and chop off whatever I don't need."

In the same way, the proverbs are used like a tool to chop off sin and wrong thinking—whatever God doesn't want in our lives. We become like an emerging sculpture that we might call *The Proverbs Thinker*. As you begin to learn about and live by the wisdom of Proverbs, think of yourself as a skillfully crafted masterpiece being fashioned by God, the Expert Artist.

Your parents don't have to be rich to leave you the treasure of wisdom.

WISDOM AND PARENTS ARE CONNECTED

God wants you to start learning wisdom from the day you're born. You may have heard all your life that you need to obey your parents' rules. It's a well-documented command from Scripture. But Proverbs tell us *why* obeying our parents is so important. Proverbs 1:8-9 says that your "father's instruction" and your "mother's teaching" will be a "garland to grace your head."

In ancient times a garland was given to a champion—a triumphant warrior or a winning athlete. The garland symbolizes finishing well in a race or a battle. This champion theme is evident in the New Testament as well. For example, the apostle Paul talks about fighting "the good fight" and "running a good race" (1 Timothy 1:18; Galatians 5:7). God wants to weave winning character traits into our lives. He uses parents to teach us how to please Him so that we may finish this life well, leave behind a good reputation, and spend eternity with Him.

We find the family-legacy theme continued in Proverbs 10:1:

A wise son brings joy to his father,
    but a foolish son grief to his mother.

One of the reasons this theme of sonship continues throughout the book of Proverbs is that we're all sons and daughters of our heavenly Father. This relationship of child to parent or guardian is the only human relationship that's truly universal. God gives us earthly parents so that we might learn how to behave toward others and our heavenly Father. As a result, when we bring joy to our earthly parents, we're also bringing glory to God, which is the ultimate purpose of our lives. It's like a two-for-one special.

If you had a transcript of the many conversations you've had with your parents over the years, it would most likely reflect the pattern that you find in Proverbs: "Studying for that test will help you make a good grade, but chatting on Facebook will earn you an F." "Obeying curfew will earn you more privileges, but coming in late will get you grounded." And the list could go on. Who knew your parents and Solomon had so much in common! Many of the proverbs are set up in a cause-and-effect format. For example:

> A man who lacks judgment derides his neighbor,
>   but a man of understanding holds his
>   tongue. (11:12)
> He who works his land will have abundant food,
>   but he who chases fantasies lacks judg-
>   ment. (12:11)

Heeding the warnings in Proverbs will transform you into someone others will view as wise. If you ignore the warnings you will come to harm.

Noah and the flood

At a recent speaking event a teenage boy came up to greet me. I was struck by how enthusiastic he was about the content of my talk. I was also struck by how freaky and messed up his hair was. It looked as if he had suffered a gigawatt-sized electrical shock.

"I can't wait to get to school and tell my friends about this evidence for creation and the reliability of the Bible," he said.

Hours earlier he hadn't been so enthusiastic. Mom told me that when she tried to wake him up, he turned over and covered his ears with a pillow. Next she jerked on his ankle, trying to pull him out of the bed.

WHY SHOULD I LISTEN TO WISDOM?

So, why should you want to seek wisdom from your parents and from the Bible? What's in it for you? Quite a bit!

Here's a summary of wisdom's benefits as described in Proverbs 3:

Benefit no. 1: A long life. Proverbs 3:1-2 tells us that wisdom will "prolong your life many years and bring you prosperity."

I was raised in the South, where we make fun of ourselves and "redneck" jokes are popular. While I don't appreciate name-calling and don't agree that all redneck slamming is positive, there is truth to be found amidst the humor. One joke goes like this: "What's the last thing a redneck says before he dies?" Answer: "Hey buddy, watch this."

"Get up," she said. "We're already late."

No response. She ran to the refrigerator and got a pitcher of water. She yanked the pillow away and poured the water on his head. (Now you know why his hair was funky.)

They made it to the church during the second session. Afterward, I thanked the mom for caring so much about her son's spiritual life that she was willing to douse his mattress with a pitcher of water.

"Yeah," said the teen, "when it comes to church, my mom is pretty hard core. But, dude, I am so glad I came."

The teen's name? Noah. Fitting, isn't it?

No one knows the hour or the day of his or her death. But in general, those who engage in foolish behavior—like the redneck—are likely to see that hour before the rest of us. This was brought to my mind recently when I talked to a friend who went to his 25th class reunion and learned that at least 10 of his classmates had already died. One had been killed in a fight, one had died from using drugs, and one had been shot by a police officer while trying to rob a grocery store.

"I hate to say it," my friend said, "but when I looked at the names printed in the reunion program, there wasn't really a surprise on the list. Every one of those kids was someone you might have guessed would either be dead or in jail before too long."

In general, wise people live longer than foolish

people. It's also a biblical and statistical certainty that every person will die one day. On that day, the wise person will find another added benefit. He or she will be comforted by this thought: *Whenever God chooses to take me, I'll be prepared to go.* The fool has no such assurance.

Benefit no. 2: Favor and a good name. Proverbs 3:4 tells us that "favor and a good name in the sight of God and man" will result from wisdom, particularly from the practice of love and faithfulness. This verse calls to mind a description of Jesus from the Gospel of Luke: "Jesus grew in wisdom and stature, and in favor with God and men" (2:52).

It takes a lifetime to build a good reputation, but only a day to destroy it.

You should never try to please people if your primary goal is to be popular. If you do, sooner or later their selfish whims will get in the way, and you may be forced to do things that are a violation of God's law. However, if you pursue wisdom, favor with people will often follow.

Benefit no. 3: A straight path. Did you know that today Egypt and Israel share a border? You can literally stand with one foot in Egypt and one foot in Israel. The distance from Cairo to Tel Aviv, where Israel's international airport is located, is less than 250 miles. In a modern jetliner, you wouldn't even get up to cruising altitude before the plane would have to begin its descent. On today's roads, you could make that trip by car in just a few hours.

Yet the Hebrew people in Moses' day wandered for decades in the exact same territory. It took them 40 years to go less than 250 miles! That shows you what a difference it makes to be on a straight path as opposed to a crooked and winding path.

One of the most well-known Bible verses summarizes this benefit:

> Trust in the LORD with all your heart
>> and lean not on your own understanding;
> in all your ways acknowledge him,
>> and he will make your paths straight.
>>> (Proverbs 3:5-6)

Benefit no. 4: The discipline of God. Rebuke is a word we don't use much anymore. It means "to scold." But the word's history enlarges and enriches its meaning. *Rebuke* also means "to beat back." Old military histories often say that one army "rebuked" the attack of another. Most of us don't like rebukes. If you're like me, you probably pouted, cried, or got in a dark mood when you were disciplined as a child.

But Proverbs 3:12 tells us that "the LORD disciplines those he loves, as a father the son he delights in." The two ideas of love and discipline fit together in a surprising way because the negative concept of discipline communicates the positive concepts of real love and intimacy. When we experience

Discipline is the bridge between good intentions and godly living.

God's discipline, we experience pain. We would, if we could, avoid that discipline, that emotional hurt. But because God loves us, He won't let us avoid it.

This tough truth can be a comfort during tough times. God's rebuke is His way of saying, "I'm not through with you yet. I have a great work in store for you, and more preparation is needed." That doesn't make the discipline any less painful to experience, but if you fully learn today's lesson, tomorrow's great work might come into view that much sooner.

Wisdom is calling

Fools despise wisdom and discipline. (Proverbs 1:7)

Wisdom calls aloud in the street,
she raises her voice in the public squares. (1:20)

For the Lord gives wisdom. (2:6)

Blessed is the man who finds wisdom. (3:13)

Get wisdom, get understanding. (4:5)

Wisdom is supreme; therefore get wisdom. (4:7)

Wisdom is more precious than rubies. (8:11)

The fear of the Lord is the beginning of wisdom. (9:10)

With humility comes wisdom. (11:2)

Wisdom is found in those who take advice. (13:10)

He who gets wisdom loves his own soul. (19:8)

Get wisdom, discipline and understanding. (23:23)

A man who loves wisdom brings joy to his father. (29:3)

The rod of correction imparts wisdom. (29:15)

3

FOOLS

how to avoid being one

Years ago my friend Beatrice had a demanding English literature teacher who loaded up the homework and writing assignments. The students speculated that the prof didn't have a life outside of work, and they thought he spent holidays planning his next lecture or quiz.

It was probably true. When the class got back from Thanksgiving break, a surprise test on John Steinbeck's short story "The Chrysanthemums" was waiting on each of the desks. The prof gave them 30 minutes for the test, and when it was over, most of the students had a lump of regret in their stomachs. They hadn't studied and didn't know how to spell *chrysanthemum* let alone answer the questions. Beatrice, however, finished the test in 15 minutes and left with confidence.

During the next class session Beatrice found she had thrown the curve by making a 96 percent.

Afterward, classmates asked her how she had known to study so hard. "I had some good advice," she said. "I always buy my textbooks used. In the margin of my literature book someone had written 'Study. Pop quiz coming after Thanksgiving break.'"

FEAR AND FOOLS

There are two ways to learn life's hard lessons. One way is to learn from your own mistakes. The other way, as Beatrice has shown us, is to learn from the experiences of others. The book of Proverbs tells us that the best way to learn is the second way—to learn from observing and listening. You really don't have to go to the school of hard knocks to get the diploma of wisdom. If you listen to and take the advice of others who are wise, you can be wise too. If you don't, then you're in danger of becoming a fOOL. Proverbs 1:7 puts it this way:

> The fear of the LORD is the beginning of
>   knowledge,
>   but fools despise wisdom and discipline.

Fear

That word *fear* is one that we North Americans stumble over. Even Christians are sometimes reluctant to embrace Proverbs 1:7 because they think that fear is negative. But this word really means "reverence." It means to have a proper appreciation for God's majesty and holiness. Think about it: God spoke the universe into existence. He is in control of the oceans, the sky, and every last star in the heavens. He knows your every thought, move, and desire. He is infinite and all-powerful and in every way perfect. You and I, on the other hand, are finite. We couldn't conjure up one tiny, single atom, let alone thousands of galaxies. You and I are dependent upon God for our very breath and life and being. We are small, insignificant creatures and far from perfect. Every last neuron in our puny brains should be pulsating this message: Fear God!

fear = respect = awe = goose bumps

That's why the "fear of the LORD is the beginning of knowledge." When you come face-to-face with God's awesomeness, you realize you have a lot to learn, and you open yourself to His truth. This attitude is called having a *teachable spirit*.

Fools

The opposite of having the fear of the Lord is being a fool—someone who isn't teachable. The words fool and foolish don't impact us strongly because we have casual associations with them. For example, we often say we are "fooling around." Also, we tend to think of a fool as being stupid or lacking intelligence. In Proverbs, however, a fool

What did Jesus say?

Jesus took the word fool seriously. In Matthew 5:21-22 He said,

> You have heard that it was said to the people long ago, "Do not murder, and anyone who murders will be subject to judgment." But I tell you that anyone who is angry with his brother will be subject to judgment.... [A]nyone who says, "You fool!" will be in danger of the fire of hell.

Wow! The people of Jesus' day didn't fool around with the word fool.

isn't someone intellectually challenged; a biblical fOOL is a person who lacks moral character.

Scripture reserves a special disdain for fOOLS.

Fool, foolishness, and folly come from Hebrew root words that imply "moral corruption."

Some variations of the word fOOL are mentioned more than 50 times in Proverbs. Most often they show the sharp contrast between wisdom and fOOLishness or the contrast between a wise person and a fOOL. In other words, being a fOOL isn't just having a shortage of wisdom; it's the *opposite* of wisdom.

TEEN WISDOM

Fortunately, wisdom isn't some secret thing God is hiding from us. "Wisdom calls aloud," Proverbs 1:20

says. Whom is it calling to? Well, primarily you!

Proverbs is directed to teens because you're close to becoming adults and having a lot of responsibilities, but you aren't experienced in life and need guidance to mature in godly ways. Being young isn't a crime, nor does it mean that teens are spiritually inferior. In the context of Proverbs, being young means that you haven't lived long enough to see the consequences of sin over time. Solomon is trying to help his son and all teens avoid mistakes so they don't have to go through a great deal of emotional, spiritual, or financial pain. He's encouraging young people to develop their moral compass early so they can begin to reap the rewards of wisdom.

Being young = being foolish

Solomon is also speaking to you because the path of folly looks alluring on first inspection. While there are exceptions, teens and young adults usually have a lot of energy and are known for being impulsive. They're likely to rush down any new road that looks inviting. Teens often don't look far enough down the road; they tend to be short-term thinkers. Solomon shows us what's at the end of a short-term path. He warns us that ruin will come to us if we follow it (Proverbs 15:10). While the way of wisdom is initially more difficult, at the end it brings forth long-term benefits and contentment.

O foolish me! Part 1

My mom Loved her sporty green Ford Mustang, which was a special gift from my dad. one summer day just after I graduated from high school, Mom offered to Let me drive the Mustang to Myrtle Beach, south carolina. soon my friend Noel and I were cruising around the popular East coast resort town, hoping to meet girls. we did. Not long afterward, the sporty Little car had four teens in it. The powerful V-8 Mustang engine added a new Level of excitement to the night.

"May I drive the Mustang?" one of the girls asked.

Deep inside, a Little voice gently said, "say no, Alex." But instead, I heard myself say, "sure!"

THREE STAGES OF FOOLISHNESS

Proverbs describes three basic types of fOOLS. If unchecked, fOOLS grow more and more morally corrupt as time passes.

The stage-one fool

This fOOL is naive and shortsighted. He doesn't look to the future. He doesn't observe cause and effect. He isn't concerned about his inner man or his character. The word simpleton comes to mind when describing fOOL number one. This fOOL goes along with the crowd and is easily swayed to experiment with evil. When he finds himself in a bad situation, he sees himself as a victim and doesn't understand how he got into such a predicament. There's hope for this fOOL because with good com-

we pulled over, and I tossed the keys to a girl I had known all of 20 minutes. Noel and I hopped into the backseat as the girls drove us around Myrtle Beach. I was about to object to the fact that we were going over 60 miles per hour in a 35-miles-per-hour zone when I noticed that we were also running a red light.

"Stop!" I shouted. "If we get pulled over, you're going to lose your license!"

The engine roared happily as we sped along. Then the girl driving shouted back, "What license?"

To be continued . . .

pany, he can be taught what is right. He's still teachable and can be scared straight.

When my friend Randy was in high school, you'd most likely have found him hunched over a computer keyboard, staring with red eyes at the monitor while playing MechWarrior. He participated in Mech competitions and placed well, which only fed his addiction. His parents set limits on the time he could play, but he sneaked onto the computer or got around their passwords to play. Eventually his grades dropped—he got a D in French—and his parents demanded he give up MechWarrior. But Randy was determined to game at all costs, continued to lie, and morphed into a stage-one FOOL.

Then he heard about a student at his high school who had been arrested by the police. Why? The teen had a gaming addiction. His parents sold the family computer and thought they had solved the problem. But their son was more foolish than they realized—he broke into a neighbor's house to get online and was caught.

Something happened in Randy's heart when he heard that story. His fool status was shattered when he humbly admitted to himself, *That could have been me.* Today he's a successful sophomore in college and has his own spending money. He also has a computer, but he chose not to purchase a MechWarrior membership. He's free from his addiction.

A wise person changes his or her mind; a fool never.

Proverbs 14:18 is the signature verse for stage-one fools: "The simple inherit folly, but the prudent are crowned with knowledge."

The stage-two fool

FOOL number two is a popoff. She talks smack. She thinks she knows everything, and instead of being pushed into evil, she jumps in feet first. She likes to cause mischief and enjoys watching others get into trouble too. She's conceited, stubborn, and pleasure-seeking. This type of fool gets into heated arguments with teachers, police officers, and parents. When this fool gets into trouble, she blames the people in authority. She won't take any personal responsibility for her actions.

Years ago I was the manager of a small Christian music store. I'd pull in to work at about noon, and the red CLOSED sign would still be dangling in the shop window. *Michelle is late again.* This employee gave me continual grief because of her tardiness and refusal to perform simple duties on schedule. I'd leave her a to-do list to organize record albums (you heard me, *albums*—12-inch vinyl LPs; they were next to the eight-track tapes!) or dust light fixtures or be sure to open at 10 A.M. When I clocked in, however, I would find she hadn't done one thing. And worse, she argued about why that was so-and-so's job and bad-mouthed the company to the other employees.

But she didn't stop there; she even made a voodoo doll. Of me. Complete with my black hair, my bushy eyebrows, and sewing pins jammed into my heart and stuck through my face. Now, let me tell you most books on management don't cover this topic, and I didn't know how to handle it at first. My gut told me that if I confronted this 45-year-old woman, she would say it was "just a joke" (see Proverbs 26:19).

Michelle needed the job and knew the store inventory better than anyone else, so I gave her one more chance. But being a stage-two fOOL, Michelle continued in her stubborn ways, complaining endlessly about me, destroying morale, and arriving late yet demanding increased wages.

The owners of the store eventually fired her, and I happened to be there on that day. Did she own up to the fOOLish consequences she had brought upon herself? Did she say she was sorry? No. Instead, Michelle came up to me—red-faced and scowling—and grabbed my shirt collar with one hand, yanking me forward. Her face was a mere five inches from mine. I could see the pores on her nose, where the makeup had caked, and the beads of sweat pooling on her upper lip. The clammy warmth of her breath bathed my cheek. Adrenaline flooded my blood-stream. *Is she going to spit at me? What do I do? I can't hurt a woman!*

Just then one of the owners, a tall man of about 60, took her gently by the elbow and said, "Now, Michelle, it's over. Nothing good is going to come of that." At the sound of his calm voice, she loos-ened her fingers as if coming out of a trance. She took a step back. The owner guided her through the door, to the parking lot, into her car, and out of my life.

I think of Michelle and other stage-two fOOLS when I read this: "The wise in heart accept com-mands, but a chattering fOOL comes to ruin" (Proverbs 10:8).

The stage-three fool

The signature sin of stage-three fOOLS is pride—they won't be taught by anyone, including God. This fOOL is beyond stubborn—he is haughty and ac-tively destructive. He has turned into a villain and is irreverent and rude. He has no true friends—even his family resents him (see Proverbs 17:21). There's no hope for this person except for a divine en-counter with God.

A stage-three fOOL'S character needs a complete transformation because he has chosen to serve evil instead of serve the God of love. He's in bondage to himself; he knows full well that his behavior is self-destructive, but he can't change it on his own. With twisted logic, he hates God for his problems.

If fOOLS won't listen to wisdom, at some point God lets them have their own way. And anytime a person chooses his or her way instead of God's wisdom, it will lead to trouble and pain.

The theme verse for a stage-three fOOL is "A man's own folly ruins his life, yet his heart rages against the LORD" (Proverbs 19:3). This next proverb also describes a hard-as-nails fOOL:

> Though you grind a fOOL in a mortar,
>> grinding him like grain with a pestle,
>> you will not remove his folly from him. (27:22)

A mortar is a bowl, and a pestle is a hard stick. For centuries people have used these tools to grind grain into meal. This metaphor shows that even if fOOLS are reduced to their smallest particles, they are still filled with folly.

Can stage-three fOOLS be helped? Perhaps. I don't believe anyone is so morally corrupt that God's love can't reach him or her. I cling to Proverbs 14:33 for hope: "Wisdom reposes in the heart of the discerning and even among fOOLS she lets herself be known." Wisdom calls out, even to fOOLS.

He who asks a question is a fool for five minutes; he who does not ask a question remains a fool forever

O foolish me! Part 2

(continued from page 31)

Then the girl recklessly driving my mom's green Mustang shouted back, "What license? I'm only 15!"

"Stop the car now!" I shouted.

The Mustang's tires squealed to a stop. The girls got out and gave me a dirty look. The one who had been driving tossed the keys to me and said, "You can have your dumb car back."

By then my friend Noel was on the pavement, bent over on hands and knees, laughing hysterically. He was panting so hard he could barely

SEDUCED BY "FOLLY"

Proverbs can't get enough of contrasting virtue with vice. Chapters 8 and 9 show us an extended metaphor about a woman called Wisdom, who is elegant and thoughtful. The other woman, Folly, is slovenly and loud. Let's take a closer look at the foolish "woman."

Folly is loud, undisciplined, and, well, determined to be bad. While the wise woman sits at the city gates with the other responsible people, Folly sits in the doorway of her own house, trying to lure the unsuspecting inside. Proverbs 9:17 likens Folly to a prostitute who offers unlawful goods:

> Stolen water is sweet;
>> food eaten in secret is delicious!

talk. "Those girls were under age, and you let them drive your mom's car!" he said. "You are so stupid!"

Yes, I was. And even Noel, who wasn't known for his common sense, recognized it. I've often thanked God that no one died that night. Fortunately I realized that I was the foolish one. I can't say I've never done anything else so stupid, but I can say it was a rude awakening that kept me from becoming a stage-two fool. Perhaps I needed to think a little more before impulsively trying to please a pretty girl

But God sees all. The consequences of our hidden deeds lead to spiritual darkness. Consider this melancholy conclusion for those who enter Folly's house:

> Little do they know that the dead are there,
>> that her guests are in the depths of the
>>> grave. (9:18)

DON'T TAKE THE BAIT

Solomon didn't spend much time describing Folly. He didn't want us to fixate on her sensationalism and lewdness. His descriptions are meant to warn us. Pretend you're a small fish—just for a minute— and you'll get the point. Imagine that Solomon is telling you and the other fishes about the dangers of a fishing hook. He doesn't describe the delicious fly or wiggling worm because he doesn't want to whet your appetite. Instead, he tells you about the hook. It's curved and pointed and sharp enough to shred your mouth. If you think only about the worm, you'll swallow it and get caught by the hook. If you fear the hook, then you won't meddle with the worm on the line, and you'll swim free.

Know fear

The fear of the Lord is the beginning of knowledge.
(Proverbs 1:7)
Do not be wise in your own eyes;
fear the Lord and shun evil. (3:7)
To fear the Lord is to hate evil. (8:13)
The fear of the Lord is the beginning of wisdom. (9:10)
The fear of the Lord adds length to life,
but the years of the wicked are cut short. (10:27)
The fear of the Lord is a fountain of life,
turning a man from the snares of death. (14:27)
The fear of the Lord teaches a man wisdom,
and humility comes before honor. (15:33)
Through love and faithfulness sin is atoned for;
through the fear of the Lord a man avoids evil. (16:6)
The fear of the Lord leads to life:
Then one rests content, untouched by trouble. (19:23)
Humility and the fear of the Lord
bring wealth and honor and life. (22:4)

4

FRIENDS

be careful whom you choose

In the 1950s a popular television program called *Leave It to Beaver* featured character Eddie Haskell, who appeared to be the all-American boy. He said "yes, ma'am" and "no, ma'am" and "That's a pretty dress you're wearing" to Mrs. Cleaver, and he always looked neat and clean. But when the adults weren't watching, Eddie Haskell's true character revealed itself, and he would do his best to get others in trouble. On the television program, the result was humor. In real life, such people leave tragedy in their wake. That's why Proverbs makes the following observations:

> Do not set foot on the path of the wicked
>   or walk in the way of evil men. (4:14)
> They eat the bread of wickedness
>   and drink the wine of violence. (4:17)

The way of the wicked is like deep darkness;
   they do not know what makes them
      stumble. (4:19)

That last verse, in particular, tells what happens when people walk "the way of the wicked." Everything may seem to be going along just fine, and then calamity will hit. Friends of yours may be using drugs and yet appear to be happy. Couples you know may be experimenting with sex and think they're being "adult" and "fulfilled." Others may cheat in school and lie to their parents, all without a flicker of remorse. But eventually their lives of foolishness will come full circle and land them in trouble, emotionally, financially, and spiritually. One day they will inevitably fall.

How can you avoid being dragged down with them? By learning how to steer clear of them in the first place.

BEWARE OF FOOLS AND ANGRY PEOPLE

Everyone gets angry, and often with justification. Anger isn't a sin, but what you do about it could be. The people to watch out for are those whose character is marked by vengeance and a lack of self-control. Hotheads spew steam everywhere they go—they are stage-two fools. Proverbs notes the following:

Do not make friends with a hot-tempered man,
   do not associate with one easily angered.
      (22:24)

A fool gives full vent to his anger,
　　but a wise man keeps himself under control.
　　　(29:11)
An angry man stirs up dissension, and a
　　hot-tempered one commits many sins. (29:22)

Teens are often characterized by churning hormones, moodiness, and intense feelings. A simple failure can feel like the end of the world, while a turn of good fortune can seem like the thrill of a lifetime. I'm not saying that anyone who has strong emotions should be shunned. For example, if a teen guy is dumped by a girl or is cut from the wrestling team, he may feel angry for a season. That's okay. But if he nurses the anger and it spills into other areas of his life on a consistent basis, then he has a lack of self-control. His anger may one day affect you, or he may become a bad example, and so you need to avoid his influence.

If you live in an area where there is gang activity, be even more choosy about your friends—especially you, young men. (Some experts estimate that 90 percent of gang members are male.) Gang members often recruit their friends to join. Remember Proverbs 16:29 if you're tempted to hang with gang members: "A violent man entices his neighbor and leads him down a path that is not good."

Gossip and mocking can also be signs of angry people. Stay away from bitter, complaining, sarcastic people who use words as weapons: "Reckless words pierce like a sword, but the tongue of the wise brings healing" (12:18).

BEWARE OF THRILL SEEKERS

Come on, confess. All of us have been with friends
and done something we know to be wrong for the
sake of fun. (I think that's an informal middle-
school graduation requirement.) Why does this
happen? Proverbs 1:10 reveals that "sinners entice
you." In other words, bad company makes sin look
good.

A friend who wants to drink and drive will *not*
say, "Hey, let's go out and get so drunk we can't see
straight, then drive around in my car until someone gets killed. After that we'll spend the next 50
years with such guilt and depression and financial
debt that we ruin our lives and the lives of those
around us." Bad company instead glosses over the
sinful parts and puts a positive spin on reckless behavior. More likely a friend with evil intent will
say, "Hey, let's go have a good time!"

Doing wrong may sound harmless, but it's not.
Proverbs 1:19 puts it this way: "[Ill-gotten gain]
takes away the lives of those who get it."

BEWARE OF SEX TRAPS

Solomon tells his readers that the way of the sexually impure goes "down to death" (Proverbs 2:18).
We shouldn't have close friendships with those
who don't follow God's rules for sexual purity.

The verses in Proverbs 2, 5, 6, and 7, as well as
Proverbs 22:14 and 30:20, refer to prostitution.

These passages imply that all sexual sin is out of bounds, not just adultery. Additionally, the warnings aren't just for men. Godly people of either gender should stay away from sexual sin of any kind.

Sexual tempters are all around you and aren't always easy to spot. If you're close friends with people who are sexually active, their values may eventually influence you. A tempter need not be the TV stereotype of a prostitute or a womanizer—a fishnet-clad woman strutting the streets while showing off her cleavage or a guy who shows up on the first date with a fistful of scented condoms. The person you most likely will be tempted by is someone you know well and with whom you share an emotional attachment. It might be your cute lab partner, your brother's friend, your math tutor, your prom date, or the coeds in the college dorms.

A seducer will make sex seem fun and oh-so attractive. Proverbs describes sexual lures as emotional as well as physical: "The lips of an adulteress drip honey, and her speech is smoother than oil" (5:3). Flattery, false promises, and seductive conversation can be a large part of the package for a tempter. The three little words "I love you" coming from a boyfriend or girlfriend can sound so innocent, yet they can often lead to sexual folly. (More on sex and romance in chapter 5.)

> If you make a fool of yourself real friends let you know you haven't done a permanent job.

SEEK OUT THE WISE

We now know who not to hang with. But who are the good guys? You can't tell by hairstyle or skin color. It doesn't matter their age or their social group or how much money their parents make. What matters is their heart. If you find a wise friend, you've found a gift. "He who walks with the wise grows wise" (Proverbs 13:20). A wise friend

- listens to correction and loves you for giving it (Proverbs 9:8-9)
- works hard (10:5)
- obeys rules and accepts authority (10:8)
- can keep a secret and guards his or her speech (10:19; 16:23)
- "wins souls" (11:30)
- "fears the LORD" (14:16)
- shows discernment and knows what's right and wrong (16:21)
- takes advice (19:20)
- has self-control (29:11)

Wise friends will have all different kinds of personalities and interests. You may find friends in unusual places—and I hope you do. Be open to finding them whenever God brings one across your path.

SEEK OUT ENCOURAGERS

We already know that the wise fear God, so the best friends are those who show by their actions that they love Jesus. A good friend "covers over an offense," "promotes love," and "loves at all times" (17:9, 17). Look for those who have a "pure heart" and whose speech is kind (22:11) so that you can be encouraged to grow closer to God.

When I was 17, I drove my father's egg van to make deliveries to local grocery stores in Greensboro, North Carolina. I became friends with Rick Davis, a teen who unloaded the eggs at the Harris Teeter store on Summit Avenue. Rick and I would double-date or just hang out and talk about music. One day I invited him to a Friday-night concert where I would be playing guitar in a band. As a lure, I assured him there would be free beer.

"Rick don't drink," he said in his peculiar way of speaking about himself in the third person.

I think my mouth dropped open so far it hit the sidewalk. That was unthinkable in our culture. Alcohol was as prevalent as water, and during my teen years I practically bathed in it. All my other friends drank, even those who went to church.

I asked him about it, and he explained, "Rick belongs to Jesus. He is now led by the Holy Spirit, not distilled spirits."

That was the first time someone had offered me an explanation about how Christians should live a different lifestyle. Rick wasn't judgmental or high and mighty. He was kind, and I could tell he was sincere about his commitment to clean living for Jesus' sake. His honest words were encouraging seeds of truth planted in my heart, and I was one step closer to becoming a Christian because of his friendship.

Talking with fools—do I or don't I?

How do we know when a fool is really just a knucklehead? How can we tell the difference between someone who is hardhearted and someone who is just ignorant or immature? When do I reach out to a person, and when do I walk away?

Proverbs 26:4-5 summarizes this tension:

> Do not answer a fool according to his folly,
>   or you will be like him yourself.
> Answer a fool according to his folly,
>   or he will be wise in his own eyes.

Some people think these verses contradict each other. In fact, I've seen this passage used on anti-christian web sites to "prove" that the Bible has errors. But in fact these verses merely capture the essence of tough relationships. You ought

SEEK OUT LOYAL FRIENDS

"As iron sharpens iron, so one man sharpens another," says Proverbs 27:17. This image is of two knife blades being drawn across each other. The friction sharpens the blades simultaneously. A good friend will help you grow in integrity and spiritual sharpness. Loyalty is also a desirable trait in a friend. Even the "wounds" from a friend are better than "kisses" from an enemy (27:6). In other words, let your friends talk to you honestly and even offer criticism. A harsh truth is better than false love from someone who doesn't care enough about you to give you straight-up advice.

When I began working at Focus on the Family in

to talk to a fool if silence would leave him "wise in his own eyes." But you shouldn't answer a fool in a way that would make you become "like him yourself." Stay away from pointless arguments.

Throughout your life you'll meet foolish, argumentative, and stubborn people. In some cases, there may be hope for dialogue and respectful conversation. In other cases the possibility of meaningful friendship is hopeless.

It takes wisdom to know when to reach out and when to walk away. God can help you learn this skill if you pray for guidance. Personally, I go after the "lost sheep" and err on the side of reaching out—at least once. I would rather be treated rudely than pass by a chance to help someone who just may listen to some wise counsel.

2004, part of my job was to write a monthly column for *Plugged In* magazine. I was really proud of my first essay, "Jesus Is the Reason for This Season," and I offered it to staff editor Tom Neven for review.

A few hours later I went back into his office. Tom swerved around in his chair. "Alex," he blurted, "about this article . . . it's *terrible!*"

Why don't you tell me how you really feel? I thought. Outwardly I laughed, but inwardly I cringed. Since then I've come to cherish Tom as a trusted friend. He's one of the smartest thinkers I've ever met. What he knows about theology and apologetics would fill an ocean. He never minces words. He never offers false encouragement. He's all no-nonsense truth. I'd rather hear about my "terrible" writing from him than get applause from anyone else.

SEEK OUT THE BEST FRIEND

Proverbs 18:24 tells about a friend who "sticks closer than a brother." I believe Jesus is that friend. The times I feel closest to Him are when I'm in a tough leadership role. In March 1995 I led a tour called 50 States in 50 Days in which I preached the gospel in every state in 50 consecutive days. During that time, I felt closer to Jesus than at any other stage in my life.

In two RVs and a Plymouth minivan, a team of five adults and nine college students drove from coast to coast. We had all kinds of logistical trials, such as getting a 40-foot RV stuck on a Utah mountaintop and having to take cold showers. We had morale issues as well. The older people on the trip complained that the college students were rude, while the college students complained that the older people were condescending. Despite the Lord's many blessings, the team wasn't always unified. The stress was so high that at one point even my wife wanted to quit the tour and fly home.

Every morning I would seek out Jesus, my best friend, in prayer. His kind encouragement and counsel and the presence of His peaceful Spirit gave me the strength to continue day by day. When my Christian friends and the other leaders let me down, Jesus was still by my side.

On the last day of the tour, CBS filmed our team as we rolled into home. All the team members were crying with joy and saying how fabulous the trip was and that they'd do it again in a heartbeat. Although I was glad they had joy, I knew for a fact that not 24 hours earlier, they had all wanted to kill each other. I was happy that day too, not just because thousands of people had heard the gospel and the tour was a success, but because I had discovered the gospel message anew. Jesus died for me, and He rose again and lives. He offers us a new life—a life that begins here on this earth when we seek His friendship and offer ours to Him.

Take my advice . . .

For lack of guidance a nation falls,
but many advisers make victory sure. (Proverbs 11:14)
The plans of the righteous are just,
but the advice of the wicked is deceitful. (12:5)
The way of a fool seems right to him,
but a wise man listens to advice. (12:15)
Plans fail for lack of counsel,
but with many advisers they succeed. (15:22)
Listen to advice and accept instruction,
and in the end you will be wise. (19:20)
Make plans by seeking advice;
if you wage war, obtain guidance. (20:18)
For waging war you need guidance,
and for victory many advisers. (24:6)

5

SEX

what does God have to do with it?

Even if you're too young to be thinking about marriage yet, it's a safe bet that you do think about sex. So it's important to understand the way God intends for you to use your sex drive so that your heart won't be scarred by sin. Let's see what Proverbs has to teach teens about sexual relationships and marriage.

Solomon mentions sex early on in Proverbs:

> [Wisdom] will save you also from the adulteress,
>   from the wayward wife with her seductive
>   words,
> who has left the partner of her youth
>   and ignored the covenant she made before
>   God. (2:16-17)

Sex outside of the safe context of marriage is to be wary of, something you need to be "saved" from. Marriage is a covenant with God. A covenant is a binding agreement and promise. If you take the covenant lightly, it negatively affects you spiritually. The mysterious Agur also commented on the dance of sexual attraction, marriage, and love. He wrote this in Proverbs 30:21-23:

> "Under three things the earth trembles,
>   under four it cannot bear up:
> a servant who becomes king,
>   a fool who is full of food,
> an unloved woman who is married,
>   and a maidservant who displaces her mistress."

Agur points out in a poetic style that when marriage goes wrong and a husband no longer loves his wife, the earth trembles, at least metaphorically. Sex should be shared in a loving, long-lasting relationship. Perhaps that's because at the creation of the world, God intended for a man and a woman to unite in body and soul and not be separated (see Genesis 2:24). And God was perfectly clear when He gave Moses and the Israelites the command "You shall not commit adultery" (Exodus 20:14).

God believes in love at first sight, second sight, third sight ... and ten-billionth sight. God created marriage for true love!

But what is adultery? A textbook definition would include voluntary sex between a married man and a woman who isn't his wife or between a married woman and a man who isn't her husband. The word *fornication* is normally used to describe sex between unmarried couples, although in the Bible the word describes any dishonoring sex acts. In Proverbs, "adultery" carries with it a broader meaning that includes all kinds of sexual sin. Just to be clear, let's define biblical sexual sin to include homosexuality, pornography, and any type of genital contact.

When people think that casual sex is okay, even satisfying, then there's a breakdown of love (Proverbs 30:20). It's more than just a melancholy topic for poets and country-western singers to write about. Sex outside of marriage is a relationship between a man and a woman gone seriously wrong. It isn't a mere sexual blunder or mistake; sexual sin attacks the hearts of the people involved. It tears apart the entire fabric of human relationships and the way God intended for men and women to be woven together spiritually.

A SAD TALE

Let me tell you about a phone conversation I once had with Carl, a longtime friend. At first he had me laughing because he couldn't keep the phone in his hand; he dropped it three times because his hands were greasy. But by the end of the conversation, I wasn't laughing anymore.

I came to find out the greasy hands were from changing his wife's flat tire—correction, his ex-wife's flat tire. Just after they had met in court to finalize the divorce, Shelby had gotten stranded and called Carl to come help her: "I didn't have anyone else to call."

Perhaps Shelby could have called the university

professor with whom she had had an affair. No, he was long gone. Carl, who had paid for her graduate-school education, found them in bed shortly after she finished her coursework. Their two-year marriage quickly dissolved.

I often wonder if Shelby regrets her moments of sexual passion with the professor. She had found love—a man willing to show it by getting both his hands and his heart dirty—and yet had frittered it away on adultery.

The devastating effects of sexual sin may not be easy to spot during high school. But those involved in it will begin to experience the emotional agony it brings in the years that follow. By the time I was midway through college, I already had friends who were having abortions; by my late 20s, many were battling in divorce court. In my 30s, marriages were falling apart because of sexual sin, but now there were children involved in the hurt. sexual sin creates pain—just ask Carl.

ON TEEN HORMONES

Teen guys spend a decade or more with—uh, how shall I phrase this?—with their sexual fires burning brightly. As they reach physical maturity, their hormone production is high. God has also wired men for action, which means that their physical daring and sexual curiosity are high as well. At the same time, teens have little experience with what works and what doesn't work, what produces good results and what produces disastrous results. All of this helps explain why accidents are the number-one cause of death among teenage males. Indeed, sexual escapades are often not exclusively or even primarily about lust. They're often about this drive to gain the experience, or dominance, that teen guys desire so strongly. If you're a guy, you should know this about yourself. If you're a teenage girl, you should know this about teen guys.

Let me be plain about one thing: None of this is any excuse to sin against God. God expects us to remain sexually pure both when it's easy and when it's difficult—no matter how many hormones are flowing.

YOU WERE MADE IN GOD'S IMAGE

So how do you deal with such a wonderful but potentially dangerous flame?

One way is to view yourself and other people as God sees you. Don't let yourself be reduced to an object—"a loaf of bread" (Proverbs 6:26) for another person to devour. Girls, please don't think of yourselves as merchandise. You don't have to spend lots of money on nails, hair coloring, jewelry, or clothes. You don't have to exercise till your body fat is below 4 percent or toast yourself in a tanning machine. Guys—same for you. Cut back on the efforts to be eye candy for the ladies.

How you present yourself will, in part, determine how people treat you. Do you present yourself as a well-packaged item for sexual consumption? It may feel nice to get the attention, but is it the right kind of attention? Girls, it's easy to get guys thinking about sex—really, you don't have to work that hard at all. But it's not so easy to get guys thinking about you as a valuable gift from God, which should be your goal for their sake as well as your own.

The world wants to devalue teens of both genders and tarnish your self-image. The world wants to make you think you're only a loaf of bread, something that will be eaten or turn stale and be thrown away. But you are made in the image of God; you were made for eternal life in a place where human souls and human bodies are cherished, not tarnished. Don't help the world with its evil plan to black out the image of God in your life. Fight against it by refusing to allow yourself to become a mere sex object.

AVOIDING SEXUAL TEMPTATION

As someone made in the image of God, choose good companions who won't ask you to do wrong (Proverbs 7:4-5). Why not be choosy about your media companions too? Studies show that teens who watch less TV are less likely to engage in sexual activity. Alcohol and drugs, which can blur the lines between what's "fun" and what's best, are also shown to promote unwise sexual behavior. For this, and many other reasons, if you stay away from drugs and alcohol, your life will go more smoothly.

But perhaps the best way is to run away from those situations that may stoke the flames of passion till they're white hot. Proverbs 6:27-28 puts it this way:

> Can a man scoop fire into his lap
>   without his clothes being burned?
> Can a man walk on hot coals
>   without his feet being scorched?

In other words, if you don't want to get burned, back away from the fire. This doesn't just include person-to-person sexual temptation but also virtual temptation like pornography. The following proverb offers another suggestion besides avoiding the fire. Don't simply run from temptation, run toward God and His Words.

> My son, keep your father's commands
>   and do not forsake your mother's teaching.
> Bind them upon your heart forever;
>   fasten them around your neck.
> When you walk, they will guide you;
>   when you sleep, they will watch over you;
>   when you awake, they will speak to you. (6:20-22)

Am I seriously saying to avoid sex by reading the Bible? Yes, that's a big part of the ongoing solution. It's God's best weapon for us to use against sin and the influence of the world's evil. Scripture is the sword of the Spirit, according to Ephesians 6:10-18.

(The following encouragement to "stand" is where the titles of my books come from.)

> Be strong in the Lord and in his mighty power. Put on the full armor of God so that you can take your stand against the devil's schemes. For our struggle is not against flesh and blood, but against the rulers, against the authorities, against the powers of this dark world and against the spiritual forces of evil in the heavenly realms. Therefore put on the full armor of God, so that when the day of evil comes, you may be able to stand your ground, and after you have done everything, to stand. Stand firm then, with the belt of truth buckled around your waist, with the breastplate of righteousness in place, and with your feet fitted with the readiness that comes from the gospel of peace. In addition to all this, take up the shield of faith, with which you can extinguish all the flaming arrows of the evil one. Take the helmet of salvation and the sword of the Spirit, which is the word of God. And pray in the Spirit on all occasions with all kinds of prayers and requests.

Reflecting on God's Words during trials works. Since sex is a matter of the soul as well as the body, this remedy works longer than a cold shower. If you feed your soul with good food, you won't be so hungry for the junk calories of sexual sin.

When trouble comes looking for you . . .

consider Joseph, the young biblical character who was sold into slavery by his 10 older brothers. when a married woman came to seduce Joseph, he made an extraordinary statement:

> no one is greater in this house than I am. My master has withheld nothing from me except you, because you are his wife. How then could I do such a wicked thing and sin against God? (Genesis 39:9)

Joseph could have gotten away with some free lovin'. He was powerful enough to keep the meeting secret or to keep the other servants from talking. But Joseph also knew that even if he could keep the woman's husband from knowing, he couldn't keep a secret from God. Joseph valued God's standards so much that he was willing to go to be punished rather than to give in to temptation.

THINK LONG-TERM

Besides the spiritual benefits, there are also practical reasons for avoiding sex outside of marriage.

I once counseled a young man who had been a Chippendales stripper in Las Vegas before he became a Christian. He confided that even though he got propositioned all the time at work, he avoided sex because of the threat of sexually transmitted

True sexual freedom is the choice to say no today so you can say yes to a great future marriage.

What did Jesus say about sex?

okay, Let's be honest. often, teLevision and movies portray immoral sexual behavior as thrilling and fulfilling. Those sexually charged images are designed to be seductive and appealing—even addicting. After reading the advice given about aduLtery in proverbs, what warning do you imagine soLomon would give about watching sex-filled media? Is it okay to "Look but not touch"? what did jesus say about that? If you don't know, check out matthew 5:28.

diseases (STDs). He and his girlfriend waited until they were married to have sex, and both agree it was worth the wait. One of the reasons is the reassurance in knowing the other is not carrying any diseases.

Here are some stats on STDs that show the long-term consequences of contracting them:

- Sexually active teens are at high risk for chlamydia, herpes, and human papillomavirus (genital warts or HPV). These STDs often have no visible symptoms at first. It may be years before signs of an STD show up in a woman's body.
- The viruses that cause herpes is permanent and will live in your body until you die. HPV, the virus tht causes cervical cancer, can also be a permanent infection.

- An STD may inhibit a female's ability to have children—ever. Many researchers equate the huge rise in infertility to rampant sexual promiscuity in our culture. Physical effects of chlamydia—a bacterial infection—are a leading cause of preventable infertility. (From www.medinstitute.org and http://std.about.com.)

WILL A CONDOM KEEP ME SAFE?

Keith Deltano is a former public-school teacher and expert on information about teens and sexual activity. Keith has spent the past 10 years giving teens throughout the United States facts they may not have heard in their public schools.

Keith gives examples of peer-reviewed studies (that means "scientist-tested") that prove condoms don't eliminate the transmission of herpes and HPV. He explains, "Herpes and HPV are skin-based diseases. They do not need the exchange of body fluid to occur in order to be contracted. The viruses can be present throughout the whole genital region. The condom only covers a portion of the genital region of one partner."

Other study findings from The Medical Institute include the following:

- If you always use condoms for vaginal sex, you will only reduce your chance of getting herpes by about half. There is no evidence that condom use reduces the risk of getting HPV through oral sex.

- Even consistent, correct condom use fails to prevent HIV infections by vaginal sex about 15 percent of the time.
- While condom use has increased over the past 25 years, the spread of STDs has likewise continued to rise.

Just to prove that stats supporting the health benefits of abstinence aren't coming just from preachers, take the government's word for it! Look for additional information from the Centers for Disease Control and Prevention (CDC); visit www .cdc.gov.

In 20 years of ministry, I've met plenty of people who became sexually active before marriage and regretted it. But I've never met anyone who said, "Oh, yes, I stayed pure until marriage, but I so wish that I had given away my virginity in high school!"

Both Christians and non-Christians relate their painful experiences with premarital sex, which impact them emotionally, spiritually, and often physically. In other words, there's a price that comes with the decisions you make.

I have yet to meet someone who handled his or her sexuality God's way and later regretted it. No one. Statistics bear this out too. Virgins who marry have the best sex lives. I'm not trying to be racy. It's just a fact that God knows what He's doing when He tells the human race how to live.

If you go looking for trouble

King David didn't wait for sexual sin to come find him; he went looking for it. Transfixed by the beauty of Bathsheba, a neighbor who bathed on the roof, David seduced her. When he found out she was pregnant, he ordered the death of her husband. David eventually repented and spent some time in spiritual anguish. The baby that he and Bathsheba conceived died. The whole story is told in 2 Samuel 11-12.

If you've been like David and sinned against God and/or another person, remember that God's mercy will be poured out to you in abundance. You can read about David's spiritual journey to healing in Psalm 51. It shows that restoration and cleansing await those with a broken heart.

NOW THE GOOD NEWS!

Is sex worth waiting for? You bet.

Proverbs 5 paints a picture of lifelong marriage in positive poetic terms. A good relationship is possible, but you have to choose it. Marriage is like a well of clear, fresh water. We're told to "drink water from . . . [our] own well" (Proverbs 5:15). When we fully love our spouse, the temptations of sexual sin are less appealing:

> A loving doe, a graceful deer . . .
>> May you ever be captivated by her love.
> Why be captivated, my son, by an adulteress?
>> Why embrace the bosom of another man's
>>> wife? (5:19-20)

As a teen you may think that you have a bit more latitude when it comes to sexual attention. And in one regard you do. You haven't yet made a lifelong promise before God to focus all your physical and emotional affections on your spouse. But odds are you'll make that commitment one day, and your ability to keep that promise will either be helped or hindered by your sexual behavior *before* you marry. When a marriage gets tough—and even great marriages get tough—the knowledge that you and your spouse share a truly exclusive and unique physical bond can help see you through those times.

Many people think about what they want in a spouse and put their energies into finding that person. I challenge you to spend your teen years becoming the kind of person that will make a "perfect" mate; put your energies into improving your own character. Ask yourself these questions: What are some of the good character traits I want in a spouse? What am I doing to develop those same qualities in myself?

On love and marriage . . .

Let love and faithfulness never leave you;
bind them around your neck,
write them on the tablet of your heart. (Proverbs 3:3)
May your fountain be blessed,
and may you rejoice in the wife of your youth.

A loving doe, a graceful deer—
may her breasts satisfy you always,
may you ever be captivated by her love. (5:18-19)
A wife of noble character is her husband's crown,
but a disgraceful wife is like decay in his bones. (12:4)
He who finds a wife finds what is good
and receives favor from the Lord. (18:22)
Houses and wealth are inherited from parents,
but a prudent wife is from the Lord. (19:14)
What a man desires is unfailing love. (19:22)
Many a man claims to have unfailing love,
but a faithful man who can find? (20:6)
He who pursues righteousness and love
finds life, prosperity and honor. (21:21)
A wife of noble character who can find?
She is worth far more than rubies.
Her husband has full confidence in her
and lacks nothing of value. (31:10-11)

6

LAZINESS

is work a four-letter word?

One way to look at the book of Proverbs is to view it as a crash course in cause and effect. In 1697 Sir Isaac Newton identified three laws of motion. Newton's third law says that "every action has an equal and opposite reaction." In the spiritual world, there's a similar law that says "every action has an inevitable consequence." The consequence to that action may be good or it may be bad, but a consequence *will* show up in your life.

With regard to sin, sometimes the consequence shows up right away as a blister does after you touch a hot coal. But sometimes it's slower and shows up as skin cancer years after a severe sunburn. Because some of the consequences of sin don't reveal themselves immediately, it's easy to believe that negative consequences can be avoided. Lazy people don't look ahead at the consequences of their actions; instead they live for the moment.

WORK IS GOOD

We live in a culture in which work is considered evil, and vacation and retirement are the true goals of work. The Bible has a completely different perspective. Work isn't a curse; it's a blessing. God gave Adam work to do before the Fall (see Genesis 2:15-19). If you have that understanding, then you can understand that Laziness toward our work or toward our family and church responsibilities is a serious matter. It's a kind of rebellion against God.

Laziness takes on many forms, and some of those forms are explicitly identified in Proverbs 6. Let's look at a few of them:

1. If you don't work unless you're commanded or required to work, that's Laziness *(verses 6:6-8).*

Go to the ant, you sluggard;
    consider its ways and be wise!
It has no commander,
    no overseer or ruler,
yet it stores its provisions in summer
    and gathers its food at harvest.

What would it be like if you got up and did your chores *before* you were asked to do them, and then looked around for extra stuff to do? Be like an ant; no one forces ants to work, but they do what needs to be done anyway because they instinctively know they'll eventually need food. It's not always pleasant to do work, but it's necessary. The wise person plans ahead, works first, and plays second.

2. If you're constantly seeking rest or distractions, that might be a sign of Laziness *(verses 6:9-11).*

How long will you lie there, you sluggard?
    When will you get up from your sleep?
A little sleep, a little slumber,
    a little folding of the hands to rest—
and poverty will come on you like a bandit
    and scarcity like an armed man.

I want to tread carefully here, because lethargy and sleepiness are sometimes signs of depression or physical illness, and I don't want to make people with health conditions feel guilty. But I also want to warn those who crave excessive naps, computer time, electronic gaming, reading, or watching movies or TV. Even a little indulgence in these areas can keep you from performing well at school or fulfilling your responsibilities at home. Giving in to constant entertainment cravings is a form of Laziness. The consequences of such behavior are bad grades, shallow friendships, poor family relationships, and more.

3. Wanting to get something for nothing is a sure sign of Laziness *(verses 6:12-15).*

A scoundrel and villain,
    who goes about with a corrupt mouth,

Liar, liar

Landing a position at Kmart as your first job out of college might not seem so great. But when Brent Hearth—a friend I hadn't seen in a couple of years—rolled up in a new car and told us about being in upper management at a local Kmart, my nearly broke college friends and I were impressed.

Brad told us that he had gone back to his home state of New Jersey and had finished his degree at Rutgers. Fresh out of business school, he came back south and landed a lucrative management job with Kmart. With Brent earning a steady paycheck and sitting behind the wheel of a new car,

> who winks with his eye,
> signals with his feet
> and motions with his fingers,
> who plots evil with deceit in his heart—
> he always stirs up dissension.
> Therefore disaster will overtake him in an instant;
> he will suddenly be destroyed—without
> remedy.

It's no accident that the passage about "sluggards" is immediately followed by a passage about a "scoundrel" and a "villain" who is constantly scheming. I'm amazed and saddened at how vulnerable people—even Christians—are to get-rich-quick schemes. Everything from stock-market and real-estate programs to multilevel marketing schemes that promise you'll be able to make money

those of us still slaving away in the "salt mines" (that's what we called our college classes) were envious.

I remember that someone in our group remarked, "Brad really got his life together quickly." Sure enough. There was only one problem, as we found out later. Brent didn't have a business degree from Rutgers. His diploma was fake, and his résumé was mostly false. When his employer inevitably found out, Brent was worse than unemployed. His laziness had brought him a smeared reputation that would take years to overcome.

while you sleep. By contrast, the apostle Paul wrote this to the church:

> When we were with you, we gave you this rule: "If a man will not work, he shall not eat." We hear that some among you are idle. They are not busy; they are busybodies. Such people we command and urge in the Lord Jesus Christ to settle down and earn the bread they eat.
> (2 Thessalonians 3:10-12)

Even if it were possible for you to get something for nothing, an understanding of Scripture should teach you that this path isn't God's way for your life. Proverbs 21:6 reminds us that "a fortune made by a lying tongue is a fleeting vapor and a deadly snare."

Diligence Pays!

Ever been tempted to quit when things got tough? Check out these famous failures:

- In the 10th grade, Michael Jordan was cut from his high-school basketball team. During his career with the Chicago Bulls, he won numerous awards. He holds the NBA highest career regular season scoring average with 30.12 points per game; in 1999, he was named the greatest North American athlete of the 20th century by ESPN.
- Beethoven's music teacher told him he was a hopeless composer. But he became one of the

DILIGENCE

Diligence is an interesting word that communicates perseverance, hard work, and industriousness—it's the opposite of Laziness. In French, the word also means a "fast coach." The implication is that an object is well made and of high quality. In Proverbs, diligence is clearly a character quality to be imitated:

Diligent hands bring wealth. (10:4)
Diligent hands will rule. (12:24)
The diligent man prizes his possessions. (12:27)
The desires of the diligent are fully satisfied.
   (13:4)
The plans of the diligent lead to profit. (21:5)

We've already talked about destructive Laziness and how it can sneak up on you "like a ban-

most acclaimed and influential composers of all
time—even though he was deaf.
- walt disney was fired from his job at a newspaper
  because he "didn't have any good ideas." However,
  his innovative film ideas led him to cofound walt
  disney studios, and he won 26 academy awards.
- winston churchill failed the 6th grade, but he became prime minister of the united kingdom during
  WWII.
- babe ruth struck out 1,330 times—but he's been
  called the greatest baseball player of all time,
  nicknamed "the sultan of swat."

dit." You can be lazy even when you're busy if
you're using your busyness as a distraction or an
excuse to keep from doing the hard things God has
given you to do in life.

Proverbs 10 takes up the theme of laziness
again, and in verse 4, we encounter a new word,
diligent:

Lazy hands make a man poor,
    but diligent hands bring wealth.

Diligence isn't a word or a quality that's considered much these days. We live in a world that de-
mands instant results. We want to lose weight *now*.
We want to get rich quick. Even the Christian
world has succumbed to this unfortunate tendency.
I can be put on the path to freedom and prosperity
by following "six simple steps." It's quick and it's

easy. Our God can and does radically and instantly transform, heal, deliver, and bless. I praise Him for that, and I rejoice when I see such radical and instant changes happen. But I've noted that most of us—even those who went from "wild" to "mild" instantly upon conversion—experience God's blessings *over time.* This is often only after diligent study of His Words and a rewarding but often slow and tough ongoing submission of our will to God.

Lazy verses

Lazy hands make a man poor,
but diligent hands bring wealth. (Proverbs 10:4)
Diligent hands will rule,
but laziness ends in slave labor. (12:24)
The lazy man does not roast his game,
but the diligent man prizes his possessions. (12:27)
The sluggard craves and gets nothing,
but the desires of the diligent are fully satisfied. (13:4)
The way of the sluggard is blocked with thorns,
but the path of the upright is a highway. (15:19)
Laziness brings on deep sleep,
and the shiftless man goes hungry. (19:15)
The sluggard's craving will be the death of him,
because his hands refuse to work. (21:25)
As a door turns on its hinges,
so a sluggard turns on his bed. (26:14)
The sluggard buries his hand in the dish;
he is too lazy to bring it back to his mouth. (26:15)

7

RIGHTEOUSNESS

is it attainable?

The book of Proverbs clearly encourages us to pursue righteousness, and it even suggests that righteous living is possible. Some form of the word right or righteous appears more than 60 times in the 31 chapters of Proverbs. Let's just look at Proverbs 10 for a smattering of them:

> Ill-gotten treasures are of no value,
>   but righteousness delivers from death.
>   (verse 2)
> The Lord does not let the righteous go hungry
>   but he thwarts the craving of the wicked.
>   (verse 3)
> Blessings crown the head of the righteous,
>   but violence overwhelms the mouth of the
>   wicked. (verse 6)
> The memory of the righteous will be a blessing,
>   but the name of the wicked will rot. (verse 7)

The mouth of the righteous is a fountain of life,
　　but violence overwhelms the mouth of the
　　　wicked. (verse 11)
The wages of the righteous bring them life,
　　but the income of the wicked brings them
　　　punishment. (verse 16)
The lips of the righteous nourish many,
　　but fools die for lack of judgment. (verse 21)
What the wicked dreads will overtake him;
　　what the righteous desire will be granted.
　　　(verse 24)

Whew! Let me stop there. The truth is that the word righteous appears six more times in this chapter alone! God clearly thinks righteousness is a good quality—a quality to be pursued and a quality that can be achieved.

So how do we reconcile these admonitions to be righteous with other passages that say righteousness isn't possible? How do we look at the shortcomings and sins in our life and still believe righteousness can be attained?

ONE WORD, FOUR DEFINITIONS

This tough question can partly be answered by digging into a bit of history. The word righteous didn't exist in English until it was created by William Tyndale for his 1526 English translation of the Bible. Tyndale was a gifted linguist who was fluent in a half-dozen languages, including the biblical languages of Hebrew and Greek. He also realized that no English word was a perfect translation for the Hebrew root word *tzedek* (used 500 times in the Old Testament) or the Greek word *diakios* (used 200 times in the New Testament).

This was a significant translation problem because these words—in the original Hebrew and Greek—can mean a variety of things. They can refer to right behavior, or they can mean making the right choice between two possibilities. The words also have technical legal meaning. A behavior is deemed to be righteous if it is in compliance with the law. And, of course, it can mean "holy," which means *perfect* or set apart for God's use.

The modern phrase "that's totally righteous, dude" takes on a whole new meaning in Proverbs.

Definition no. 1: right behavior

Think of it this way: If I'm in a store and I'm tempted to steal something, I can make the "righteous" decision not to steal, and in doing so, I have chosen righteousness by conforming my behavior to God's standards.

Definition no. 2: making a righteous choice

I can be at the store with money jingling in my pocket, and then I look out the window and see a young girl without shoes. She is trudging through

The million-dollar choice

The scene was Ground Zero, New York City, about 48 hours after the terrorist attacks on the twin towers. I was working with a well-known ministry and helping with relief efforts.

A newscaster for WMCA, a New York Christian radio station, wanted to interview me just outside the hotel where I was staying. It was a career-highlight opportunity for me, plus I wanted the ministry to get some publicity. Just as the nicely dressed newscaster and the man with the microphone came over to interview me, I noticed an old man trying to cross the buzzing intersection of Avenue of the Americas and 30th Street. No one else besides me seemed to be paying attention to him or his white cane. Especially not the cars zooming by with no regard for pedestrians or the speed limit. If he puts a foot into that street, he'll be flattened by a taxi or a truck, I thought. I asked the reporter if she would wait while I helped him. She looked at her watch. "Listen, I've got to go on the air here in just a minute. Decide, you can't do both."

the snow on her way home from school. The "righteous" choice is to forgo buying my food and instead purchase shoes for the cold girl before she gets frostbitten.

Definition no. 3: conforming to the law

If I make the righteous choice not to steal repeatedly and consistently, I might even be called a "righteous" person because I follow the law on a daily basis. I can also follow the moral law and

The choice was before me: radio interview or save an old man's life. In other words: seek worldly fame or humble myself and do the righteous thing. I thanked the reporter but declined the interview. I hurried over to the man and gently took his elbow. "Let's cross together," I suggested. Once safely on the other side of the street, the man asked some questions about who I was and what I was doing in New York (my southern background gives me a decidedly non-New York accent). I told him about the ministry I was with at the time.

"In 1957, they changed my life," he said. "I'm going to give a million dollars because a nice young man like you helped me across the street." Sure enough, a few days later a million-dollar check arrived at the ministry. The righteous choice was definitely the right choice. As Proverbs 11:18 says: "He who sows righteousness reaps a sure reward."

spend my money righteously by giving part of my earnings to the poor. But that righteousness doesn't make me perfect. My righteousness doesn't reconcile me to God.

The Pharisees in Jesus' day spent a lot of time trying to be righteous by studying the law of Moses and following rules. They were proud of themselves, but they were missing the whole point (see Matthew 23:13–36). Today, we call that kind of follow-the-rules thinking *legalism.*

Definition no. 4: righteousness because of Jesus

Righteous is used to describe a person who has become a Christian. The Christian is okay in God's book because Jesus' sacrifice on the cross atoned for (made legally void) his or her sin.

The cumulative total of all my righteous decisions can't lift me to the level of true holiness or the righteousness of God. That kind of righteousness can come only by faith in Jesus. That's why salvation and righteousness are gifts. We can't earn them—they are transferred to us by Jesus by way of the cross.

ENCOURAGEMENTS TO RIGHTEOUS OR GODLY LIVING

This word study helps us see that there's no contradiction in the Proverbs passages with any other sections of Scripture. It may seem obvious to say that God would want us to live our lives in a godly manner. Certainly this idea underlies much of Proverbs. So while all of Proverbs is about *what* we should do in life, a big chunk of Proverbs—16:1–22:16–is an encouragement or a guide for *how* we should live righteous and holy lives before God in a fallen world. To follow this guidance we must look at a key concept in these chapters: desire.

The word *desire* is an interesting one. It often conjures up notions of lust, greed, and want. "I want it, and I want it now" is a powerful idea in pop culture. Clearly, longing and desire are hardwired into the human experience.

Let's take a look at Proverbs 19:22, an interesting verse on this subject: "What a man desires is unfailing love." The implication here is that none of our longings and desires have a chance of fulfillment outside of God's love, which is the only love that is truly unfailing. In fact, we could say that our only true desire is a desire for God and that all other desires come from that desire.

For example, a desire to get married or for a good relationship with your parents comes from a God-given desire for loving relationships.

Adultery is a twisted way of acting out the desire for God. Greed for money is a perversion of the God-given desire for a secure relationship or safety.

It is exciting to realize that our deepest desires often intersect with God's plan for our life, thus giving us an opportunity for the making of a righteous choice. I have met Christians of all ages who were willing to put aside long-cherished plans for something better—God's plan. And there was joy in it!

I think about Blake, a software engineer who left a mega-bucks career to enter seminary. Working part time while he pursues a theology degree, Blake is earning only a fraction of what he did as a software developer. "I can honestly say I am the happiest I've ever been," he said. "I am a part of something that will matter in the lives of people forever."

Justice according to Proverbs

Righteousness also includes the notion of justice. This concept can be defined as "holding ourselves up to an unchanging standard," or God's standard of righteousness.

> [Acquire] a disciplined and prudent life,
>   [do] what is right and just and fair. (Proverbs 1:3)

> For [God] guards the course of the just
>   and protects the way of his faithful ones. (2:8)

> Then you will understand what is right and just
>   and fair—every good path. (2:9)

> All the words of my mouth are just;
>   none of them is crooked or perverse. (8:8)

> I walk in the way of righteousness,
>   along the paths of justice. (8:20)

> The plans of the righteous are just,
>   but the advice of the wicked is deceitful. (12:5)

> The lips of a king speak as an oracle,
>   and his mouth should not betray justice. (16:10)

> A wicked man accepts a bribe in secret
>   to pervert the course of justice. (17:23)

Said another way, our desires are either worship or idolatry. If that's true, then what desires are pleasing to God? What desires are truly manifestations, or inklings, of a longing for God?

Psalm 73:25 says, "Whom have I in heaven but you? And earth has nothing I desire besides you." The yous in this passage refer to God. Do the things and people and goals that fill up your life over-

It is not good to be partial to the wicked
or to deprive the innocent of justice. (18:5)

A corrupt witness mocks at justice,
and the mouth of the wicked gulps down
evil. (19:28)

To do what is right and just
is more acceptable to the Lord than sacrifice.
(21:3)

When justice is done, it brings joy to the righteous
but terror to evildoers. (21:15)

Evil men do not understand justice,
but those who seek the Lord understand it
fully. (28:5)

By justice a king gives a country stability,
but one who is greedy for bribes tears it
down. (29:4)

The righteous care about justice for the poor,
but the wicked have no such concern. (29:7)

Many seek an audience with a ruler,
but it is from the Lord that man gets justice. (29:26)

shadow your desire for God, or is He tops in your life? Living a righteous and holy life in this fallen world must begin with allowing God to transform our desires into His righteous desires.

8

SELF-CONTROL

why it matters so much

If you were to read Proverbs in Hebrew (the original language), you would notice repeated uses of the words that mean "discipline" and "correction." Sometimes these passages imply the use of physical punishment, such as in Proverbs 22:15 and 23:13-14, but more often they speak of learning, training, and growth through self-control. If we're smart, we'll impose such discipline on ourselves.

As you read Proverbs, imagine that you're a fortunate pupil listening to a gifted teacher. Your instructor repeatedly informs you that not only should you *love* discipline, but it's *stupid* to resist it (12:1). Why is your teacher asking you to pay attention to the proverbs? Proverbs 22:19 gives the answer: "So that your trust may be in the LORD."

You're not only supposed to trust Scripture for yourself, but also to share with others. One of the favorite verses of apologists is 1 Peter 3:15: "Always be prepared to give an answer to everyone who asks you to give the reason for the hope that you have." The basic idea is this: Be able to explain what you believe and why.

Proverbs 22:21 contains a similar thought. The writer of Proverbs is "teaching you true and reliable words, so that you can give sound answers to him who sent you." Yes, God's Words are "true and reliable." In a world of endless opinions, it's great to know that humanity does have a God-given vault of *truth.* Believers are to accept God's revealed truth—and to live it, love it, know it, share it, and show it. Day in and day out, in all situations, we're Christ's representatives.

An apologist is someone who defends the Words of God.

To be any good at this multifaceted assignment, you'll need a good textbook. And years of practice. On this lifelong mission for God, some days you'll do better than others. Some days you'll blow it. God may seem distant for long periods at a time; then God will surprise you with a stunning revelation.

The first step on the road to godly SeLf-control is turning your ears and heart toward God's Words.

"GET THE BUFFALO MEAT LOAF! YOU'LL LOVE IT LIKE I DO."

Meat loaf made from buffalo has never been on my must-have list for a meal. But I once ordered it at a restaurant, after my host had urged me about three times to "go on, give it a try." I was being interviewed for a series of speaking engagements, and it became clear to me that my host was very proud of his city and wanted me to experience the great things that made it unique. One of these things was, apparently, buffalo meat loaf. My host watched as I took the first few bites, eager to know that I liked this dish that was new to me. My host seemed pleased that I was willing to try it, and I ended up getting the speaking gig. Buffalo is not my favorite, but choking it down was a small price to pay.

More than one corporate leader has told me that he learns about new recruits by taking them out for a nice meal. For good or for ill, one impression that we leave with a person may render significant consequences later on. Our manners and the ways in which we conduct ourselves tell others much about us. self-control is not just the ability to stop doing "bad" things but it is the ability to do the right thing or to conform ourselves to better serve those in power, and ultimately God.

Employers have told me of people who missed out on opportunities because they ate too much, talked too much, or offended the boss by ordering the most expensive thing on the menu. A little bit of self-control would have landed them the job or the promotion.

Even in Solomon's time, it was important to have a good handle on social cues. Proverbs 23 says this: "When you sit to dine with a ruler, note well what is

A prayer and a pay raise

one summer during college I got a job selling cars at a dealership in Greensboro, North Carolina. I was trained by the manager, a hard-nosed, cursing swindler—he fit the stereotype of a dishonest car salesman in every detail. He even encouraged me to flatter people by telling them they looked good riding in the car and to lie by saying I'd bargained with the manager on the customer's behalf when I hadn't.

He took me to lunch one day, and I wanted to thank God for my food, so I said a blessing over our meal. I explained I was a new Christian and that I hoped that didn't bother him. Days later when I got

before you, and put a knife to your throat if you are given to gluttony" (verses 1-2). (Not a literal knife! Remember, this is a literary device like the examples in chapter 1. This means do whatever it takes to stop overeating.) Use good manners, be a gracious guest, and display self-control. People will take note, and the impression you make will be positive.

DESIRES AND SELF-CONTROL

Plans. Goals. Agendas. Aspirations. Appetites. Lusts. Desires. What do you want from life? Are you able to control your desires, or do they control you? Are your desires righteous, as we discussed in chapter 7? People throughout history have pondered the way in which selfish inner cravings have

my next paycheck I noticed a small increase in pay. I asked the payroll clerk why, and he said, "The boss has been in this business 40 years, and no one has ever had the guts to pray over a meal with him. He gave you that raise because he thinks you have moxie."

The message of this story is not to say a prayer and you'll get a pay raise; I've never received another financial bonus from praying at a restaurant even though I thank God for my food before every meal. The message is to do what's right and to honor God no matter the social obstacles.

overpowered the morals of even the strongest of individuals. Twenty-three hundred years ago a famous Greek philosopher named Aristotle said, "I count him braver who overcomes his desires than him who conquers his enemies; for the hardest victory is over self."

Proverbs, too, has a lot to say about keeping our wants in check. Proverbs 23:4 says, "Do not wear yourself out to get rich; have the wisdom to show restraint." Clearly, verses like this one are a warning about *greed.*

But there are many other potential snares waiting for us: gluttony, stinginess, envy, drunkenness, dishonesty, sexual immorality, to name but a few. Think about someone you know whose desires are out of control. Not pretty, is it? The writer of Proverbs isn't trying to beat us down with excessive preaching. Learning self-control is all about the care of your *soul.* This stuff matters big-time.

Whether the assignment is to eat veggies before reaching for dessert or finish homework before playing on the PlayStation3, a life skill you'd better learn early is how to prioritize, which means having self-control. Making discipline a habit and forcing yourself to exercise self-restraint yields great benefits later on. This reminds me of the words found in Hebrews 12:11: "No discipline seems pleasant at the time, but painful. Later on, however, it produces a harvest of righteousness and peace for those who have been trained by it."

CONTROLLING OUR WORDS

We live in a world where everyone makes promises. Advertisements make all kinds of promises to get our attention and to get us to buy things we don't really need. We make promises to each other, some that we don't keep. "Let's get together," we might say to someone, and then we never call to schedule a time. Your mom asks you to talk to someone, and the next time the subject comes up, she asks whether you've done it. You tell her, "I left a voice mail, but I haven't heard back yet." Now, assuming you really did leave a voice mail, and you weren't lying to her about that, you've still dodged her question. She didn't ask if you had tried to do something; she asked if you had done it.

I remember the story of a little boy who took a few

cookies from his mother's cookie jar. She later asked him, "Did you take a cookie from the cookie jar?"

He quickly answered, "No!"

His mother knew, though, that someone had been in the cookie jar, and that someone could only have been him. So she warned, "Don't lie to me, or you'll get in even worse trouble."

He finally answered, "I didn't lie. You asked if I took a cookie. I didn't take *a* cookie. I took five!"

Perhaps answers like this are why the New Testaments says, "If anyone considers himself religious and yet does not keep a tight rein on his tongue, he deceives himself and his religion is worthless" (James 1:26). Our words are often the most difficult thing to control.

Whether we like to admit it or not, all of us lead lives full of little lies. In fact, researchers at the University of Vienna in Austria released a study in 2001 that said we lie many times a day just to "cope with reality." Men lie more than women, but not by much. Men lie about their cars; women about shopping. "All my maintenance is up-to-date," a man who has car trouble might say. "I got a great deal on these shoes," said one woman who was a compulsive spender.

Mainly we lie to make other people think we have better judgment than we have, or that we're not as messed up as we really are. Sometimes we come to believe our lies.

Unfortunately, churchgoers aren't much better than the rest of the world when it comes to telling the truth. Here's one particularly telling example:

For years the Gallup organization has been asking people if they regularly attend church. Usually the way they ask the question is something like this: "Have you attended a religious service in the past seven days?" Typically, between 40 and 45 percent of Americans will answer yes to that question. However, other studies that get people to fill out calendars and diaries of how they spend their time suggest that only about 20 to 25 percent of Americans actually attend church. In other words, as many as half of American churchgoers actually lie about going to church!

By learning to govern what we say and especially to avoid lies, we are building self-control that matters. It also matters that we don't spread anger with our words but instead have self-control when we want to lash out. Proverbs warns:

> When words are many, sin is not absent,
>   but he who holds his tongue is wise. (10:19)
> A man of knowledge uses words with restraint,
>   and a man of understanding is even-tempered.
>   (17:27)

INTEGRITY IS ALWAYS IN STYLE

When I was in high school, there was a drive-in movie theater in town. Spending money was scarce, and the three dollars per person it cost to get inside seemed an exorbitant price to pay. So as a "clever" teen, I would ride in the trunk of my friends' cars so that I could get inside. Today, I'm ashamed that I sacrificed my integrity for three dollars, and I confess I wasn't living for God, so saving money seemed more important than honesty. But what's worse is I didn't even think of it as wrong—it was just a game. I had no moral self-control.

Times haven't changed much. In a 2008 survey of more than 29,000 high schoolers from across America, 64 percent admitted to having cheated on a test within the past year. Thirty percent confessed to having shoplifted something during the past 12 months. Of the same group, 93 percent of the students felt "satisfied with their personal ethics and character." Despite evidence indicating the absence of integrity, 77 percent believed that they were "better than most people I know."

Even way back in Solomon's day, ethics mattered. self-control that yielded honesty was central to society. Centuries come and go, cultures rise and fall, and gadgets get updated. That's about it. But truth, morality, and ethics *remain.* In every era of history, the pursuit of what is honest and true has demonstrated maturity and godliness. What's real and what's right don't change. Those who build their lives on what God says is good go the distance. What foundation are you building on right now?

DISCIPLINE: THE KEY TO GREATNESS

A famous violinist, about to perform for an eager audience, was asked the secret of his musical prowess. The maestro explained that years ago he put himself on a regimen of "planned neglect." He said, "I thought about all of the things I could be doing but which would hinder my musical progress. I wrote down what they were and planned to neglect these things."

That, my friends, is commitment. I'm sure it wasn't easy. But such commitment will take you places—like the stage of Carnegie Hall in New York City.

You might be thinking that commitment, discipline, and self-control aren't fun. You may be thinking, *If I don't get to do* _____ (fill in the blank), *I'll miss out!* I used to play that card on my parents. Yep. "Missing out." If you live a life of godliness and discipline and self-control, you'll miss out on some things. Things like mental anguish, feelings of guilt, and stress caused by bad decisions. Missing out on some things isn't so bad. Be one who wisely misses some avoidable pains and the poverty endured by those who don't learn to motivate themselves to control themselves and do what's best.

Discipline

We can't earn our salvation, but discipline is a way we can achieve wisdom and holiness. Proverbs has much to say about the power of a disciplined and orderly life:

For attaining wisdom and discipline . . . (1:2)

Fools despise wisdom and discipline. (1:7)

My son, do not despise the Lord's discipline. (3:11)

The Lord disciplines those he loves. (3:12)

He will die for lack of discipline. (5:23)

The corrections of discipline are the way to life. (6:23)

He who heeds discipline shows the way to life. (10:17)

Whoever loves discipline loves knowledge. (12:1)

He who ignores discipline comes to
poverty and shame. (13:18)

He who spares the rod hates his son, but he who loves
him is careful to discipline him. (13:24)

A fool spurns his father's discipline. (15:5)

Stern discipline awaits him who leaves the path. (15:10)

He who ignores discipline despises himself. (15:32)

Discipline your son, for in that there is hope. (19:18)

Folly is bound up in the heart of a child, but the rod of
discipline will drive it far from him. (22:15)

Do not withhold discipline from a child. (23:13)

Buy the truth and do not sell it;
get wisdom, discipline and understanding. (23:23)

9

RELATIONSHIPS

can't we all just get along?

One of my favorite jokes goes like this: A man was stranded all alone on an island for 20 years. When he was finally found, his rescuers discovered that he had built a town on the island. He lived in a nice home, and there were buildings you might find in any small town: a bank, a store, even a church. In fact, there were two churches. When his rescuers asked him why he had built two churches, the castaway pointed to one of the churches and said, "I couldn't stand the guy who went to that church."

This man couldn't even get along with himself!

The bottom line is that people are tough to get along with because people are wicked. That's a hard fact to digest because we don't want to think of ourselves as wicked. But tragically it's true. The apostle Paul put it this way:

Hezekiah who?

Hezekiah was a king of Judah. He was one of the most prominent kings in all of scripture, and one of the best. Consider this description of him:

> Hezekiah trusted in the Lord, the God of Israel. There was no one like him among all the kings of Judah, either before him or after him. He held fast to the Lord and did not cease to follow him; he kept the commands the Lord had given Moses. (2 Kings 18:5-6)

Hezekiah brought both civil and religious reforms to Judah, and one of those reforms was to encourage obedience to the Law of Moses and to the wisdom of the past. That wisdom included the sayings of Solomon, which is why Hezekiah had his men compile them.

> We know that the law is spiritual; but I am unspiritual, sold as a slave to sin. I do not understand what I do. For what I want to do I do not do, but what I hate I do. (Romans 7:14-15)

But even though we're wicked, God still wants the best for us here on earth not just in heaven. That's one of the reasons the Bible gives us instruction on how to live well and peaceably today.

Proverbs 25 gives us advice on how to get along with others. This chapter, as well as chapters 26 through 29, were compiled by King Hezekiah's senior leaders.

We're going to learn about relationships

by taking an in-depth look at Proverbs 25 as well as some teaching from Jesus that builds on the proverbs. In this chapter I'll be looking at several passages in which both the Proverbs and the New Testament teach us how to handle reLationships. We'll divide this discussion into four sections:

reLationships with kings
(Proverbs 25:1-7; Luke 14:8-11)
reLationships with neighbors
(25:8-20; Luke 10:27; Matthew 18:15-17)
reLationships with enemies
(25:21-23; Matthew 5:43-45)
reLationships with yourself
(25:24-28; Matthew 7:3-5)

RELATIONSHIPS WITH KINGS

Everyone can be a leader, but not everyone is the king—or the president or the CEO or the governor or whatever you call the number-one position in your organization.

That's why the first seven verses of Proverbs 25 are so valuable. If you happen to be the king, good advice is hard to come by. You have no peers. Most people will tell you what you *want* to hear, not what you *need* to hear. In such situations, advice from Proverbs 25 is golden.

If you are *not* the king, this advice is perhaps even more precious because it helps you understand the mind of a king and make yourself invaluable to him (or her). The first piece of information referring to kings is as follows:

> It is the glory of God to conceal a matter;
>> to search out a matter is the glory of kings.
>>> (Proverbs 25:2)

This verse has always puzzled me, so I got some help from the famous commentator Matthew Henry. He wrote that this passage refers specifically to sin. It's the "glory of God" to cover sin, to put it away, to forgive. But we humans—especially those in leadership roles—are to reveal sin, to search it out, to uncover it. Such searching tells the people that the king loves justice. It's an incentive for the people to avoid evil because the relentless power of the king will find them out.

"Honesty is the best policy. If I lose mine honor, I lose myself."
—Shakespeare

Verses 4 and 5 advise kings to "remove the wicked" from their presence. Not only are kings to seek out sin, but they also are to make sure their friends and advisers have good character too.

Consider the Watergate conspiracy of the 1970s that brought Richard Nixon's presidency to an end, landed many of his advisers in jail, and shook the world's confidence in our government. All of it started with a simple burglary. The attempt to hide the crime ultimately brought down "all the president's men," as one famous book chronicling the event put it. After Watergate, a saying started going around Washington: "It ain't the crime; it's the cover-up that'll get you." This story is an example of why leaders should seek to uncover injustice and be careful not to commit crimes themselves.

The following verses teach us the value of humility and how we should approach a king, including the King of Kings.

> Do not exalt yourself in the king's presence,
>   and do not claim a place among great men;
> it is better for him to say to you, "Come up here,"
>   than for him to humiliate you before a noble-
>   man. (25:6-7)

You hear an unmistakable echo of this proverb in one of Jesus' parables, which is found in Luke 14:8-11:

> When someone invites you to a wedding feast, do not take the place of honor, for a person more distinguished than you may have been invited. If so, the host who invited both of you will come and say to you, "Give this man your seat." Then, humiliated, you will have to take the least important place. But when you are invited, take the lowest place, so that when your host comes, he will say to you, "Friend, move up to a better place." Then you will be honored in the presence of all your fellow guests. For everyone who exalts himself will be humbled, and he who humbles himself will be exalted.

The computer network guru who knew too much

when I became president of southern evangelical seminary in 2006, I interviewed a computer network technician, a young woman who was related to my barber. she wanted to impress me and began showing me all the stuff she could do for the school's network. after a few minutes, she logged onto some pay-only sites and showed me that with the right sequence of clicks, the protection could be overridden, and I could access the sites for free. wow, I thought, this woman knows a lot, too much

The lessons here are unmistakable. Godly leadership requires purity of heart and humility of spirit. And you must be completely open to seeing and telling the truth, whatever that truth may be.

Do you hang out with those who have bad habits or do wrong things? If so, ask yourself what King Solomon would have you do. How humble and teachable are you? (This isn't a trick question!) Do you seek to help and serve others, or do you expect people to serve you?

RELATIONSHIPS WITH NEIGHBORS

The book of Proverbs has quite a lot to say about relationships with neighbors. References to neighbors are sprinkled throughout—with four of them in chapter 25. There are more than 100 references to neighbors and how we should relate to

about the wrong things. As a Leader, I couldn't afford to work with a technician who was proud of the fact she could break into other companies' sites without paying. No matter how good she was with computers, she had some unethical habits I couldn't overlook. I hired another computer network technician to work for the school, one with better character and who I could be sure wouldn't try to cheat the school or worse, ruin the seminary's reputation for honesty and integrity.

them in Scripture. In fact, a reference to neighbors is in the most important law God gave to us:

> "Love the Lord your God with all your
> heart and with all your soul and with all
> your strength and with all your mind";
> and, "Love your neighbor as yourself."
> (Luke 10:27)

Proverbs 25 is helpful because it gives advice about *how* to obey God's commandments. Verses 7-10, in particular, give us guidelines for resolving conflict:

> What you have seen with your eyes
>   do not bring hastily to court,
> for what will you do in the end
>   if your neighbor puts you to shame?

If you argue your case with a neighbor,
>   do not betray another man's confidence,
> or he who hears it may shame you
>   and you will never lose your bad reputation.

As we live in community with our neighbors, conflicts and differences will occur. When this happens, we should go to our neighbors first, quietly, and not make the matter public. Going to court should be a last resort. Be warned, however, that in the process of going to your neighbor, you might find out that you're wrong. In short, these verses advise humility and mercy, even if you think you're in the right and the other person is in the wrong.

In Matthew 18:15-17 Jesus echoes this advice on how to treat a "brother" who "sins against you"—do it in private and with respect. We fallen human beings, however, often make simple things complicated and complicated things simple. Even with these clear instructions to show humility and mercy toward our brothers, sisters, and neighbors, we want to quibble with God. For example, in the New Testament one of the teachers of the law asked Jesus, "Who is my neighbor?" The underlying question really was this: Must I be nice to *everyone*?

This question prompted Jesus to tell the story of the good Samaritan, which is sometimes called the parable of the good neighbor. The parable is about a man who is beaten by robbers and helped by a Samaritan after two others pass the victim by without helping. After Jesus finished the story, He said to the lawyer,

> "Which of these three do you think was a neighbor to the man who fell into the hands of robbers?"
>
> The expert in the law replied, "The one who had mercy on him."
>
> Jesus told him, "Go and do likewise." (Luke 10:36-37)

So, "go and do" all the things mentioned in this chapter of Proverbs. Do them because these proverbs specifically command you to, but also do them because the "greatest commandment" tells you to "love your neighbor as yourself." Such a command can only mean that you show the same understanding and mercy to others that you hope to receive yourself.

RELATIONSHIPS WITH ENEMIES

Showing mercy toward brothers, sisters, and neighbors is one thing, but what do we do about our enemies? God's Words counsel that we also show love toward them. Don't believe it? Keep reading.

> If your enemy is hungry, give him food to eat;
>   if he is thirsty, give him water to drink.
> In doing this, you will heap burning coals on
>   his head, and the LORD will reward you.
>   (Proverbs 25:21-22)

God doesn't want us to live in conflict even with our enemies. As Christians we should recognize the main reason that God desires peace among people: Jesus died for all, even our enemies. Our enemies are precious to God. That's a hard thought to get our minds around, yet it's true.

Godly relationship advice is simple to understand but difficult to act on: Love everyone, period.

But what about people who are truly evil? What about countries that are enemies of life and liberty? God loves evil people and evil countries, too. It's important that we remember this overarching truth: People, tribes, groups, and even nations that we may consider our enemies are in fact humans just like us—humans, that is, who are living under the curse of sin. As a friend of mine once said, "They aren't truly the enemy; they're in bondage to the Enemy."

Jesus might have had Proverbs 25 in mind when He said this:

> You have heard that it was said, "Love your neighbor and hate your enemy." But I tell you: Love your enemies and pray for those who persecute you, that you may be sons of your Father in heaven. (Matthew 5:43-45)

At this point in our study of Proverbs, you should be realizing that the laws of the Old Testament and the New Testament are really the same law—the law of love.

RELATIONSHIPS WITH YOURSELF

Proverbs 25 closes with some practical advice that is all but self-explanatory. These verses are interesting and offer valuable advice—and sometimes they're even wryly humorous. Consider verse 24 to see what I mean:

> Better to live on a corner of the roof
>   than share a house with a quarrelsome wife.

Even such an obvious statement as this can benefit from some additional commentary. This verse, for example, takes on additional meaning when you learn that it was common for servants to live on the roofs of the people they served, often in lean-to shelters that barely offered protection from the weather. Yet being a lowly servant in an uncomfortable hut is better than being a nobleman living in luxury with a quarrelsome wife.

The last verse of this chapter is interesting and instructive because it points out that God expects us to take responsibility for our lives:

> Like a city whose walls are broken down
>   is a man who lacks self-control. (verse 28)

It's important to remember that in the day of Solomon walls represented safety and security. A city with broken-down walls offered no security, so peaceable folk would often flee such cities. Broken walls allowed evil people to enter the city at will. So it is with those who lack self-control; their character walls are broken. They'll soon find their better instincts fleeing them and their worst tendencies taking control. Such people lack peace in their spirit and aren't able to help others—even those they love—in times of need.

Take responsibility. Give love.

A chapter dealing with various kinds of reLationships fittingly ends with personal responsibility. At the root of all healthy dealings with others is the need for a healthy spirit, a health that begins with personal self-control.

Jesus notes in Matthew 7:3-5 that a person must worry about his or her own sin before looking to correct or help others.

> Why do you look at the speck of sawdust in your brother's eye and pay no attention to the plank in your own eye? How can you say to your brother, "Let me take the speck out of your eye," when all the time there is a plank in your own eye? You hypocrite, first take the plank out of your own eye, and then you will see clearly to remove the speck from your brother's eye.

If you want to have a good reLationship with others, begin by making sure that you are monitoring your own actions and that they are in accordance with God's wisdom.

Neighborly Wisdom

Do not plot harm against your neighbor,
who lives trustfully near you. (3:29)
With his mouth the godless destroys his neighbor,
but through knowledge the righteous escape. (11:9)
A man who lacks judgment derides his neighbor,
but a man of understanding holds his tongue. (11:12)
The poor are shunned even by their neighbors,
but the rich have many friends. (14:20)
He who despises his neighbor sins,
but blessed is he who is kind to the needy. (14:21)
A violent man entices his neighbor
and leads him down a path that is not good. (16:29)
A man lacking in judgment strikes hands in pledge
and puts up security for his neighbor. (17:18)
The wicked man craves evil;
his neighbor gets no mercy from him. (21:10)
Do not testify against your neighbor without cause,
or use your lips to deceive. (24:28)
If you argue your case with a neighbor,
do not betray another man's confidence. (25:9)
Seldom set foot in your neighbor's house—
too much of you, and he will hate you. (25:17)
Like a club or a sword or a sharp arrow is the man who
gives false testimony against his neighbor. (25:18)
Like a madman shooting firebrands or deadly arrows
is a man who deceives his neighbor and says,
"I was only joking!" (26:18-19)

If a man loudly blesses his neighbor early
in the morning, it will be taken as a curse. (27:14)
Whoever flatters his neighbor
is spreading a net for his feet. (29:5)

10

LEADERSHIP

are you a good or a bad example?

Frank Reich had good reason to be frustrated at the start of his National Football League career. He had been a star quarterback for the University of Maryland Terrapins, but he was relegated to a backup role with the Buffalo Bills in the NFL. Game after game would go by, and he would never get on the field. He had been in the league four years before he got his first start, when the starting quarterback (and future Hall of Fame player) Jim Kelly was injured. But Reich, a committed Christian, knew that even though he was a second-string quarterback, he was also part of a team. He kept himself prepared, mentally and physically, and when he had his chances to play, he made the most of them.

Because of that attitude, Reich may be the most famous backup quarterback in football history. It's certain that one particular game will be remembered. That game came in the 1993 play-offs against the Houston Oilers. Injuries on the Buffalo Bills' roster had taken out not only Jim Kelly but other key players on the team. Reich found himself and his team in serious trouble as the second half started. They were down 28-3 against one of the best defenses in the league. To make matters worse, Reich threw an interception early in the second half, and the score became even more lopsided: 35-3.

But then a whole series of things started going right for Frank Reich and the Buffalo Bills. They scored one touchdown. Then another. Then another. With three minutes remaining, Buffalo took the lead 38-35. Houston managed to score a field goal to tie the game at 38 and send it into overtime. Then the Bills kicked a field goal in overtime to win a game that has been called the greatest comeback in football history.

Reich later went into full-time Christian ministry, and he speaks often about the comeback to church and corporate groups. One of the things he always says about that win is this: "I may have been the Leader of the team, but it was the team that won. Not me." He also says, "If I had waited until that day to prepare for that challenge, I would have failed. Life doesn't let you pick when the challenges come. You can't know that. But you can choose to be prepared for them whenever they come."

THE UNMENTIONED VIRTUE

Did you know that you can look all day long in your Bible, and you can refer to your concordance (a book that alphabetically lists words in the Bible), but you won't find the word Leadership any-where? It's simply not there in most versions. Yet one of the great themes of Proverbs is that follow-ers of God are to be Leaders. Followership and Leadership are two sides of the coin of God's realm.

We're all Leaders whether we like it or not. Right now there are people in your life who are watching you and asking these questions: Do I want to be like this person—or not? Can I learn from this person—or not? Can I serve, or be served by, this person—or not? Your life is ei-ther an example or a warning. If you're a human being, you're a Leader.

Bible study + concordance = eureka!

Let's take a look at a few verses from Proverbs that shed some light on the issue:

> The wise in heart accept commands,
>> but a chattering fool comes to ruin. (10:8)
> He who heeds discipline shows the way to life,
>> but whoever ignores correction leads others
>>> astray. (10:17)
> Diligent hands will rule,
>> but laziness ends in slave labor. (12:24)
> A wise servant will rule over a disgraceful son,
>> and will share the inheritance as one of the
>>> brothers. (17:2)

In these verses we see some important aspects of Leadership. For example, we see that diligence

Who's smarter than a king?

A sad tale of poor leadership describes the life of
Solomon's son Rehoboam. when Rehoboam took
the throne, he despised the wise counsel of old
men and instead listened to the advice of his
peers. This led to the fall of the united Israelite
kingdom, and the 12 tribes were split into two
groups. (see 1 Kings 12).

and wisdom are important qualities in becoming a
Leader (10:8; 12:24). We also learn that true
Leadership is a function of wisdom, not of position or station in life (17:2). A Leader must also be
a follower or one who accepts commands (10:8).

There's no question that everyone is a Leader,
whether he or she wants to be one or not. The only
real questions about Leadership are these:
Where will I Lead? Will I Lead people toward life,
or will I Lead them astray? (See Proverbs 10:17.)

Leadership and preparing to Lead are strong
themes at the end of Proverbs. Just like the son for
whom Solomon wrote the proverbs, all of us are in
some ways created to be kings. God told humankind to have dominion over the earth, to Lead the
earth. The exact meaning of *dominion* has been the
subject of many books. But I think it means, at a
very minimum, that we are to exercise control
over ourselves. And as we learn what it takes to
exercise self-control, God and the natural order
that He ordained often allows us to take on greater
responsibilities.

A FINAL CALL FOR HUMILITY

Even if you're not much of a Bible scholar, you probably know a bit about some of the Bible's main characters. Adam and Eve. Noah. Moses. King David. Solomon. Jesus. Paul. These names probably mean something to you.

But how about Agur? Besides reading about him in this book, had you even heard of him? If the answer is no, then you're not alone. The first verse of Proverbs 30 is one of the most mysterious in Scripture:

> The sayings of Agur son of Jakeh—an oracle:
>   This man declared to Ithiel, to Ithiel and to
> Ucal.

No one has come up with a truly satisfactory explanation for the identity of these four people. In fact, we aren't even sure these are the actual words. If you divide up the Hebrew letters in a slightly different pattern, the phrase "to Ithiel, to Ithiel and to Ucal" means "I am weary, O God, I am weary, O God, and faint."

Whatever the meaning of verse 1, it's clear that God and Solomon want us to hear what Agur has to say to Leaders. Solomon could have said, "I'm the wisest guy there is, and so I don't have to listen to anyone else." Not only would that have been prideful; it would also have been foolish for him to discount the advice of others. On the other hand,

Solomon couldn't accept the advice of just anyone. But for some reason Solomon, with God's direction, valued Agur's perspective and put it in his collection of proverbs.

Leaders can learn something of value from Solomon as we read the proverbs of Agur: We should heed the advice of the wise men and women God has put around us.

Humility is essential to learning leadership

Agur's chapter 30 begins with a cry of unworthiness. The words show that he has humility, which is the beginning of learning.

You have humility as well. After all, you're reading this book because you think that Proverbs might have something to teach you. The first step toward Leading others is an admission that there's something you don't know. The second step is believing that someone else may know what you don't know and that you can learn from this person. So when I read verses 2-4, I don't hear someone who is depressed or in despair or ignorant or foolish; I hear someone who is in the proper frame of mind and condition of spirit to learn:

Humility is taking pride in God and others.

I am the most ignorant of men;
  I do not have a man's understanding.

I have not learned wisdom,
  nor have I knowledge of the Holy One.
Who has gone up to heaven and come down?
  Who has gathered up the wind in the hollow
    of his hands?
Who has wrapped up the waters in his cloak?
  Who has established all the ends of the earth?
What is his name, and the name of his son?
  Tell me if you know!

ADVICE TO KINGS FROM A KING

So chapter 31, the final chapter of Proverbs, is the final set of instructions for anyone who would exercise Leadership. The authorship of this chapter is ascribed to King Lemuel who was writing an oracle, or prophecy, from his mother. Like Agur, no one knows for sure who King Lemuel is, but many scholars think it is a pen name for Solomon. Here's Solomon's special name, *Jedidiah*, given to him by God through the prophet Nathan, means "beloved of God." This is a close connection.

Are you a good leader? Look at who is following you. Good leaders will have good people following them.

Additionally, this advice parallels facts that we have about Solomon's life and might have been written by his mother, Bathsheba. It warns against strong drink, which Solomon had let consume him at times (Ecclesiastes 2:3). It also warns against opening his heart to the wrong women, which we've already mentioned led to his downfall (1 Kings 11:1–4).

No matter who wrote it, this final chapter of Proverbs, the capstone of the book, includes instructions about two things: Leadership and advice to a young man for picking a wife.

A PICTURE OF THE WISE WOMAN

It's important for us to remember that Proverbs 31 isn't primarily a chapter about wives (though it most certainly is about wives) or even primarily about women (though it certainly is about women, too). It's primarily about character, specifically about noble character. Even though Solomon wrote and compiled the proverbs for the benefit of his son, we nonetheless take them to have universal applicability. So this description about the "wife of noble character" has lessons for us all.

That said, let me also say plainly that this last chapter of Proverbs reflects great understanding about the marriage relationship and what both the man and the woman uniquely and separately bring to a relationship. It's worth noting that this section of Proverbs 31 asks a question that implies that the answer is unattainable: "A wife of noble character who can find?" (verse 10).

As we read this passage, we get the sense that the writer was describing the woman he wished he had found but never did. That sense is heightened by verse 11:

Her husband has full confidence in her
    and lacks nothing of value.

The next half-dozen verses (12–17) are particularly interesting to me because they paint a picture
that is at odds with stereotypes of the "perfect
wife." Whether the stereotype of the ideal wife is
the career woman, stay-at-home mom, or the
beauty-parlor doll, the woman described in Proverbs
31 defies all categorization. She's all of the above,
none of the above, and much more. Consider verses
13–19:

She selects wool and flax
    and works with eager hands.
She is like the merchant ships,
    bringing her food from afar.
She gets up while it is still dark;
    she provides food for her family
    and portions for her servant girls.
She considers a field and buys it;
    out of her earnings she plants a vineyard.
She sets about her work vigorously;
    her arms are strong for her tasks.
She sees that her trading is profitable,
    and her lamp does not go out at night.
In her hand she holds the distaff
    and grasps the spindle with her fingers.

This is no idle woman. She works both inside
and outside the home. She is tough and physically

strong. She works even after the sun has gone down. ("Her lamp does not go out at night.") But why does she work? For personal gain or to get ahead or to "keep up with the Joneses"—whatever that might have looked like in the society of three thousand years ago? Is she looking for independence or power or control?

No. She does what she does for others. Verse 20 makes this plain:

> She opens her arms to the poor
>   and extends her hands to the needy.

She doesn't just help the poor, of course. Her children benefit so much from her that they "arise and call her blessed; her husband also, and he praises her" (verse 28).

Proverbs and all of Scripture speak to every phase of our lives. As an example, let me take a passage—and a topic, for that matter—that we haven't spent much time on during our discussion of Proverbs. The topic is caring for the poor, and the passage is in the Leadership section of Proverbs 31:

> Speak up for those who cannot speak for
>   themselves,
>   for the rights of all who are destitute.
> Speak up and judge fairly;
>   defend the rights of the poor and needy.
>   (verses 8-9)

A child might read this verse and put it into practice by looking after a younger sister or a friend who is being picked on by a class bully. A politician could certainly find in this verse a command to speak up for the underclasses of society. Lawyers and judges would also find a particular instruction here: Judge fairly. And none of us can turn away from that last statement: "Defend the rights of the poor and needy."

This passage is like a finely cut diamond that reveals a different flash and gleam no matter what angle it's viewed from.

> *"Watch your thoughts, for they become words. Watch your words, for they become actions. Watch your actions, for they become habits. Watch your habits, for they become character. Watch your character, for it becomes your destiny."*
> *—author unknown*

ENDING WHERE WE BEGAN

Proverbs 31 is both a fitting and, in some ways, ironic chapter with which to end this book. Proverbs, after all, was written to a son, yet it ends with the description of the ideal woman. That, of course, makes sense, because marriage—the creation of a new family, with all the responsibilities that go along with it—is perhaps the most significant graduation event, marking the transition from adolescence to adulthood.

Get wisdom for all eternity

Because I'm an evangelist at heart, I simply cannot bring this book to a close without asking if you have made the wisest decision of all—saying yes to Jesus. We get a taste of this calling in Proverbs 3:5-6.

> Trust in the Lord with all your heart
> and lean not on your own understanding;
>
> in all your ways acknowledge him,
> and he will make your paths straight.

If you want your paths straight for all eternity, I encourage you to enter into a personal relationship with Jesus. Being a follower of Jesus begins with receiving Him as your Forgiver, Leader, and Lord. It is soul commitment that goes beyond mere head knowledge. Christianity is a lifelong wisdom adventure with God, but it must begin with your turning to Christ, which includes belief, faith, and trust.

Jesus is as near as a prayer. If you would like to

But toward the end of Proverbs 31, we encounter a verse that brings the entire chapter, the entire book, and our discussion together, full circle. We said that Proverbs 1:7 was the theme for entire book:

> The fear of the Lord is the beginning of knowledge,
> but fools despise wisdom and discipline.

Now, at the end of the book, we encounter the same idea, this time used to describe the ideal woman:

welcome Him into your life right now, I encourage you to pray something like this:

Dear Lord Jesus,

I know that I have sinned and have wandered from you. I turn from my sins, and I ask you to forgive me. I do not want to live foolishly any more. I believe that you are who you claimed to be—the Son of God. I believe that you died on the cross for my sins and rose from the grave to give me eternal life. I acknowledge you as my Lord and Savior. Please help me to grow in spiritual wisdom.

If you made a decision to become a Christ-follower, let us hear from you. Or if you have other questions about making a commitment to Jesus Christ, please contact Focus on the Family:

CALL 800-A-FAMILY (232-6459)
or visit www.fousonthefamily.com
and click on the "Faith" menu.

Charm is deceptive, and beauty is fleeting;
but a woman who fears the LORD is to be
praised. (31:30)

In these words, we see not only what quality this ideal Proverbs 31 woman should have—a fear or awe of the Lord—but we're also left to conclude, I believe, that while the entire book of Proverbs was written and compiled for Solomon's son, it's also written for us all. Let this page not be "the end" but the beginning of an exciting new chapter in your life of service to a holy, loving, and merciful God.

Dos and don'ts from Proverbs

1. Don't rob the poor. (22:22-23)
2. Don't associate with hot-tempered people. (22:24-25)
3. Don't obligate to pay back someone else's debts. (22:26-27)
4. Do apply yourself and be skillful. (22:29)
5. Don't eat like a glutton. (23:1-3)
6. Don't be materialistic. (23:4-5)
7. Don't eat with, nor acquire the habits of, a selfish person. (23:6-8)
8. Don't waste time conversing with a fool. (23:9)
9. Don't avoid disciplining your child. (23:13-14)
10. Do be wise and forthright. (23:15-16)
11. Don't be jealous of sinners; do fear God. (23:17-18)
12. Do be wise when making goals. (23:19)
13. Don't hang out with drunks and gluttons. (23:20-21)
14. Do listen to your father and mother. (23:22-23)
15. Do make your parents happy by being wise. (23:24-25)
16. Do follow your father's advice and avoid the adulterous woman. (23:26-28)
17. Don't be a drunkard. (23:29-35)
18. Don't be jealous of sinners. (24:1-2)
19. Do be wise when building a house. (24:3-4)
20. Do seek wise counsel. (24:5-6)
21. Don't be a fool when you are serving the community. (24:7)
22. Don't plan to sin. (24:8-9)

23. Do cultivate endurance and become strong. (24:10)

24. Do assist others because God is aware how we treat those who need help. (24:11-12)

25. Do seek wisdom because it is a delicacy, as sweet as honey. (24:13-14)

26. Don't rob the house of a godly person (and I'll add "don't rob anybody!"). (24:15-16)

27. Don't celebrate when trouble comes to an enemy. (24:17-18)

28. Don't be jealous of the sinful. (24:19)

29. Do fear God, fear the king, and avoid rebels who bend the rules. (24:21-22)

30. Don't show favoritism in legal matters. (24:23-25)

31. Do give honest answers. (24:26)

32. Do exercise diligence in your business ("cultivate your field"). (24:27)

33. Don't commit perjury in court. (24:28)

34. Don't seek revenge for yourself. (24:29)

35. Don't be lazy or you'll fall into financial ruin. (24:30-34)

A PROVERBS READING GUIDE

listening to the wisdom of God

All over the United States, an odorless, colorless gas seeps through soil and into the air. The gas, called radon, is caused by the breakdown of a radioactive element. If a house is built over ground that releases too much radon, the poisonous gas is trapped in crawl spaces, cellars, and basements. To get rid of it, homeowners must install a special pump that keeps the air moving so radon doesn't build up to toxic levels. If a house in a contaminated zone doesn't have the pump, the poison will condense to dangerous levels. Those who breathe it day after day are at high risk for lung and stomach cancer.

Radioactive radon is like the sin in our culture; it's difficult to detect but can lead to serious problems if left unchecked. If we ignore the sin problem, the effects of it will eventually cause cancer in our souls.

The best way to get rid of sin on a daily basis is to install a purifying pump for our souls. The pump will move out the poison before it reaches dangerous levels. That "pump" is Scripture. And the book of Proverbs is specially designed to help you avoid sin in many practical matters.

Follow this daily reading guide to help you breathe in the pure wisdom of Proverbs. Each set of verses covers one chapter. There are 31 chapters, so you can read one every day, and you'll finish the book in a month. The lines provided with each of the following sections are for you to create a personal wisdom journal. Who knows, like Solomon, maybe you'll be passing along the collection to your family and friends one day.

Proverbs 1

_____

_____

Proverbs 2

_____

_____

Proverbs 3

_____

_____

Proverbs 4

_____

_____

Proverbs 5

_____

_____

Proverbs 6

_____

_____

Proverbs 7

_____

_____

Proverbs 8

_____

_____

Proverbs 9

_____

_____

Proverbs 10

_____

_____

Proverbs 11

_____

_____

Proverbs 12

_____

_____

Proverbs 13

_____

_____

Proverbs 14

_____

_____

Proverbs 15

_____

_____

Proverbs 16

_____

_____

Proverbs 17

_____

_____

Proverbs 18

_____

_____

Proverbs 19

_____

_____

Proverbs 20

_____

_____

Proverbs 21

_____

_____

Proverbs 22

_____

_____

Proverbs 23

_____

_____

Proverbs 24

_____

_____

Proverbs 25

_____

_____

Proverbs 26

_____

_____

Proverbs 27

_____

_____

Proverbs 28

_____

_____

Proverbs 29

_____

_____

Proverbs 30

_____

_____

Proverbs 31

_____

_____

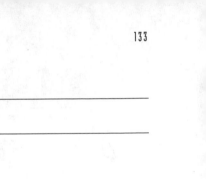

FOCUS ON THE FAMILY®

Welcome to the Family

Whether you purchased this book, borrowed it, or received it as a gift, we're glad you're reading it. It's just one of the many helpful, encouraging, and biblically based resources produced by Focus on the Family® for people in all stages of life.

Focus began in 1977 with the vision of one man, Dr. James Dobson, a licensed psychologist and author of numerous best-selling books on marriage, parenting, and family. Alarmed by the societal, political, and economic pressures that were threatening the existence of the American family, Dr. Dobson founded Focus on the Family with one employee and a once-a-week radio broadcast aired on 36 stations.

Now an international organization reaching millions of people daily, Focus on the Family is dedicated to preserving values and strengthening and encouraging families through the life-changing message of Jesus Christ.

Focus on the Family MAGAZINES

These faith-building, character-developing publications address the interests, issues, concerns, and challenges faced by every member of your family from preschool through the senior years.

| FOCUS ON THE FAMILY® MAGAZINE | FOCUS ON THE FAMILY CLUBHOUSE JR.® Ages 4 to 8 | FOCUS ON THE FAMILY CLUBHOUSE® Ages 8 to 12 | FOCUS ON THE FAMILY CITIZEN® U.S. news issues |

For More INFORMATION

ONLINE:
Log on to
FocusOnTheFamily.com
In Canada, log on to
FocusOnTheFamily.ca

PHONE:
Call toll-free:
800-A-FAMILY
(232-6459)
In Canada, call toll-free:
800-661-9800

Rev. 12/08

More Great Resources
from Focus on the Family®

Stand:
Core Truths You Must Know for an Unshakable Faith

by Alex McFarland
Ready to know why our core beliefs are important to everyday life? Alex's first book *Stand* will get you off the roller coaster of doubt

and on to solid ground. By understanding the purpose of Jesus Christ's life, death, and resurrection, you'll be ready to stand as a light in our dark world. Paperback.

Stand Strong in College

by Alex McFarland
How can you prepare for the academic, social, emotional, and spiritual challenges you'll face in college? This book will help you identify false worldviews and discern God's voice. Every student can *Stand Strong* and face the future with confidence. Paperback.